Limited Company Accounts (IAS)

Workbook

NVQ Accounting Unit 11
AAT Diploma Pathway Unit 11

David Cox

Derek Street

osborne
BOOKS

Published by Osborne Books Limited
Unit 1B Everoak Estate
Bromyard Road
Worcester WR2 5HP
Tel 01905 748071
Email books@osbornebooks.co.uk
Website www.osbornebooks.co.uk

Design by Richard Holt
Cover image from Getty Images

Printed by the Bath Press, Bath

British Library Cataloguing in Publication Data
A catalogue record for this book is available from the British Library

ISBN 1 872962 88 2

Contents

practice examinations

appendix

index of international accounting standards

About this Workbook

This revised Workbook follows the order of the Tutorial text and provides a wealth of practice material for students. The authors have taken care to amend all the assessment material so that it accurately reflects the change to international accounting standards, using the formats and terminology that students will expect to find in their examinations. International accounting standards are now required for all Unit 11 examinations, on both NVQ and Diploma qualification routes.

Acknowledgements

The authors wish to thank the following for their help with the editing and production of the book: Jean Cox, Michael Fardon, Mike Gilbert, Rosemarie Griffiths and Claire McCarthy. Special thanks go to Roger Petheram of Worcester College of Technology and Chris Waterston of Leeds Metropolitan University for reading, checking and advising on the development of the text. The publisher is indebted to the Association of Accounting Technicians for its generous help and advice to the authors during the preparation of this text, and for permission to reproduce assessment material.

Authors

David Cox, the lead author of this text, is a Certified Accountant with more than twenty years' experience teaching accountancy students over a wide range of levels. Formerly with the Management and Professional Studies Department at Worcester College of Technology, he now lectures on a freelance basis and carries out educational consultancy work in accountancy studies. He is author and joint author of a number of textbooks in the areas of accounting, finance and banking.

Derek Street, who has compiled a number of the Workbook Activities and Assignments, has had over fifteen years' experience of teaching accountancy students, including the AAT qualification at all three levels. His lecturing experience has been gained at Evesham College of FE, Gloucester College of Arts and Technology (GLOSCAT) and North East Worcestershire College.

How to use this book

Limited Company Accounts (IAS) Workbook is designed to be used alongside Osborne Books' *Limited Company Accounts (IAS) Tutorial* and is ideal for student use in the classroom, at home and on distance learning courses. Both the *Tutorial* and the *Workbook* are designed for students preparing for assessment for Unit 11.

Limited Company Accounts (IAS) Workbook is divided into three sections: Workbook Activities, Assignments and Practice Examinations.

Workbook Activities

Workbook Activities are self-contained exercises which are designed to be used to supplement the activities in the tutorial text. The Activities – some of which are adapted from AAT Examination tasks – provide useful practice for students preparing for assessments. They have been carefully designed to reflect the style of task which students can expect to find in their assessments.

Assignments

The Assignments in this section, which include some adapted from AAT Examination tasks, are intended to be used as students progress through the course, to consolidate learning and to provide practice in Examination technique. The chapters of the tutorial text covered by each Assignment are listed in the Assignment Introduction on page 70.

Practice Examinations

Osborne Books is grateful to the AAT for their kind permission to reproduce AAT examination questions. These practice Examination tasks have been carefully revised to reflect the change to international accounting standards, which are now assessed by AAT in all their Unit 11 Examinations.

Answers

The answers to the Activities, Assignments and Examinations in the *Workbook* are available in a separate *Tutor Pack*. Please contact the Osborne Books Sales Office on 01905 748071 for details.

www.osbornebooks.co.uk

Visit the Osborne Books website, which contains Resources sections for tutors and students. These sections provide a wealth of free material, including downloadable documents and layouts and assistance with other areas of study.

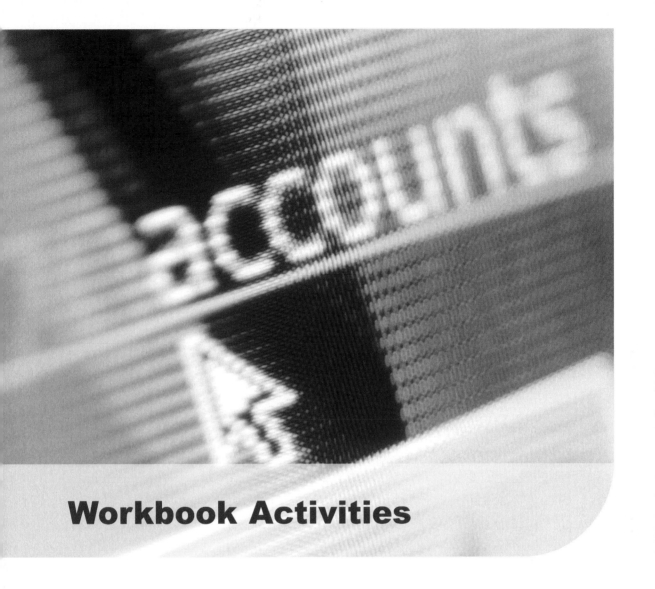

Workbook Activities

This section contains activities which are suitable for use with the individual chapters of *Limited Company Accounts (IAS) Tutorial* from Osborne Books.

Note that blank photocopiable pro-formas are included in the Appendix – it is advisable to enlarge them up to full A4 size.

1 PURPOSE OF FINANCIAL STATEMENTS

1.1 Which one of the following is not a private sector organisation?

(a)   a local authority

(b)   a private limited company

(c)   a partnership

(d)   a public limited company

1.2 Which one of the following statements is correct?

	Assets	Liabilities	Equity
	£	£	£
(a)	30,500	10,250	40,750
(b)	17,250	31,500	14,250
(c)	22,300	10,100	16,500
(d)	26,450	10,850	15,600

1.3 Which one of the following is commonly the most important objective for the private sector?

(a)   environmental issues

(b)   profit

(c)   training for employees

(d)   increased market share

1.4   Which one of the following statements best describes the accounting concept of going concern?

(a)   Income and expenses are matched to the same time period in which they relate.

(b)   The business entity will continue to trade for the foreseeable future.

(c)   When a business produces its financial statements it should always adopt a conservative figure for profit and/or the valuation of its assets.

(d)   Items with a low value should not be reported separately in the financial accounts.

1.5   The International Accounting Standards Board's *Framework for the Preparation and Presentation of Financial Statements* states that:

> *"The objective of financial statements is to provide information about the financial position, performance and changes in financial position of an entity that is useful to a wide range of users in making economic decisions."*

Illustrate this objective by selecting one external user and one internal user of financial statements and showing how each uses financial statements to make economic decisions

1.6   Briefly explain the following concepts which are used in accountancy:

(a)   Materiality

(b)   Going concern

(c)   Accruals

1.7   The *Framework for the Preparation and Presentation of Financial Statements* has been developed by the International Accounting Standards Committee (now Board). Explain the reasons for the need to develop such a framework.

1.8 The accounting equation of a business is as follows:

Assets £2,000 – Liabilities £1,200 = Equity £800

The business subsequently makes two transactions:

(1) it purchases inventories (stock) for £250 cash, and

(2) it sells the inventories purchased in (1) on credit for £350

Required:

(a) Explain what each of the terms 'assets', 'liabilities' and 'equity' means.

(b) Explain the effect of each of the two transactions on the elements in the balance sheet.

(c) State the accounting equation for the business after the two transactions have taken place.

(d) Draft a simple income statement for the two transactions.

(e) Give an example of a user who might be interested in an income statement. Describe one type of decision which might be made by the user based on information in the income statement.

1.9 Distinguish between 'economic decisions' and 'stewardship' in relation to financial statements.

2 INTRODUCTION TO LIMITED COMPANY ACCOUNTS

2.1 The abbreviation PLC stands for:

    (a)   public limited company

    (b)   private limited company

    (c)   personal liability company

    (d)   public liability clause

2.2 A PLC in the UK must have a minimum authorised share capital of:

    (a)   £100,000

    (b)   £75,000

    (c)   £50,000

    (d)   £25,000

2.3 Which document issued by a limited company forms the constitution of the company, regulating its affairs to the outside world?

    (a)   Articles of Association

    (b)   Memorandum of Association

    (c)   Annual return

    (d)   Corporate report

2.4 Reserves in a company belong to the:

    (a)   ordinary shareholders

    (b)   directors

    (c)   debenture holders

    (d)   preference shareholders

2.5 Identify the advantages of forming a limited liability company.

2.6 List the five main clauses of the Memorandum of Association.

2.7 Explain the difference between the nominal value and the market value of shares.

2.8   The following trial balance has been extracted from the books of account for Gooch PLC as at 31 May 20-5:

	Dr £000	Cr £000
Administrative expenses	210	
Distribution costs	190	
Wages and salaries	350	
Directors fees	200	
Motor and travel costs	100	
Rent, rates and insurance	150	
General expenses	120	
Issued share capital		500
Trade receivables	500	
Cash and cash equivalents	50	
Share premium account		100
Buildings:		
At cost	1,000	
Accumulated depreciation at 1 June 20-4		100
Plant and equipment:		
At cost	800	
Accumulated depreciation at 1 June 20-4		320
Purchases	900	
Revenue		2,500
Trade payables		400
Inventories at 1 June 20-4	110	
Retained earnings at 1 June 20-4		760
	4,680	4,680

Additional Information

•   Inventories at 31 May 20-5 are valued at £130,000.

•   The tax liabilities based on the profits for the year are £80,000.

•   The company's authorised and issued share capital consists of 1,000,000 ordinary shares of 50p each.

•   The company operates the following policy with regard to depreciation:

   –   Buildings 2% per annum on cost

   –   Plant and equipment 20% per annum on cost

REQUIRED

Task 1

Prepare the company's income statement (including a statement of the change in retained earnings) for the year to 31 May 20-5.

Task 2

Prepare the company's balance sheet as at 31 May 20-5.

Task 3

Explain briefly how the balance on the share premium account arose.

Task 4

List three differences between ordinary shares and preference shares.

2.9 The following trial balance has been extracted from the books of Rafter plc for the year to 31 March 20-1:

	Dr	Cr
	£000	*£000*
Administrative expenses	1,300	
Advertising expenses	10	
Authorised and issued share capital:		
ordinary shares of £1 each		500
Bad debts written off	50	
Cash and cash equivalents	400	
10% Debenture loan		2,000
Debenture interest (to 30 September 20-0)	100	
Trade receivables and trade payables	1,500	2,300
Share premium account		185
Directors' fees	350	
Distribution costs	570	
Non-current assets: at cost	6,000	
accumulated depreciation (at 1 April 20-0)		800
General expenses	80	
Interim dividend paid on 1 October 20-0	40	
Purchases	5,600	
Retained earnings (at 1 April 20-0)		435
Rent, rates, and insurance	630	
Revenue		11,810
Inventories (at 1 April 20-0)	1,400	
	18,030	18,030

Additional information

1   Inventories at 31 March 20-1 are valued at £1,200,000.

2   The non-current assets are to be depreciated at a rate of 10% per annum on cost.

3   After the preparation of the above trial balance, it was discovered that £70,000 was owing for rent and rates, and £50,000 had been paid in advance for insurance.

4   The tax liabilities based on the profits for the year are £120,000.

5   The remaining debenture interest due in the year is to be accrued.

REQUIRED

Prepare the financial statements of Rafter plc for the year ended 31 March 20-1.

2.10   The following trial balance has been extracted from the books of Squire plc as at 31 March 20-1:

	Dr	Cr
	£000	£000
Cash and cash equivalents	230	
Commission paid	6	
Interest paid	30	
Non-current assets at cost	1,100	
Non-current assets accumulated depreciation (at 1 April 20-0)		400
Office expenses	40	
Office rent, rates, heat and light	170	
Office wages and salaries	450	
Retained earnings (at 1 April 20-0)		208
Dividends paid	100	
Purchases	1,200	
Revenue		2,800
Share capital (ordinary shares of £1 each)		1,500
Inventories at 1 April 20-0	200	
Trade receivables	1,180	
Trade payables		178
Vehicle delivery expenses	320	
Communication expenses	60	
	5,086	5,086

Additional information

The following items have not been taken into account in preparing the above trial balance:

1   Inventories at 31 March 20-1 are valued at £250,000.

2   Rates paid in advance at 31 March 20-1 amounted to £5,000.

3   Rent due at 31 March 20-1 amounted to £15,000.

4   The tax liabilities based on the profits for the year are £120,000.

5   Depreciation is charged on the non-current assets at a rate of 20% on cost (on the assumption that there is no residual value) using the straight-line method.

REQUIRED

Prepare the financial statements of Squire plc for the year ended 31 March 20-1.

2.11 The following information relates to Placate PLC a company which buys and sells electrical goods.

The company's year end is the 30 June each year, and the Assistant Accountant has provided you with the draft accounts on an extended trial balance (see next page).

In order to complete the accounts corporation tax due on this year's profit has been calculated at £8,430.

REQUIRED

Task 1

Prepare the company's income statement (including a statement of the change in retained earnings) for the year ended 30 June 20-6 and a balance sheet as at the same date.

Task 2

What are the main differences between a capital reserve and a revenue reserve on a limited company balance sheet?

EXTENDED TRIAL BALANCE   name: Placate PLC   date: 30 June 20-6

Description	Trial balance Dr £	Trial balance Cr £	Adjustments Dr £	Adjustments Cr £	Income statement Dr £	Income statement Cr £	Balance sheet Dr £	Balance sheet Cr £
Revenue		425,000				425,000		
Purchases	207,500				207,500			
Salaries and wages	15,000		2,600		17,600			
Motor expenses	13,500				13,500			
Rates	10,100			1,100	9,000			
Light and heat	6,950		350		7,300			
Cleaning and maintenance costs	4,250				4,250			
Advertising	3,600				3,600			
Inventories	21,500		26,000	26,000	21,500	26,000	26,000	
Trade receivables	20,500						20,500	
Provision for doubtful receivables		3,160	1,110					2,050
Decrease in provision for doubtful receivables				1,110		1,110		
Cash and cash equivalents	7,500						7,500	
Trade payables		43,500						43,500
Bank loan		50,000						50,000
Buildings – cost	515,000						515,000	
Fixtures and fittings – cost	25,000						25,000	
Motor vehicles – cost	80,000						80,000	
Share premium account		26,500						26,500
Buildings – accumulated depreciation		50,000		25,750				75,750
Fixtures & fittings – accumulated depreciation		7,500		5,000				12,500
Motor vehicles – accumulated depreciation		40,000		20,000				60,000
Retained earnings		100,500						100,500
Depreciation – Buildings			25,750		25,750			
Depreciation – Fixtures & fittings			5,000		5,000			
Depreciation – Motor vehicles			20,000		20,000			
Dividends paid*	30,000				30,000			
Returns inwards	4,500				4,500			
Directors salaries	60,000				60,000			
Returns outwards		6,900				6,900		
General expenses	9,650				9,650			
Insurance	12,250			2,250	10,000			
Loan interest	6,260				6,260			
Accruals				2,950				2,950
Prepayments			3,350				3,350	
Share capital		300,000						300,000
Profit for the year					3,600			3,600
* to be deducted from retained earnings								
	1,053,060	1,053,060	84,160	84,160	459,010	459,010	677,350	677,350

3 PUBLISHED ACCOUNTS OF LIMITED COMPANIES

3.1 Which one of the following expenses will not be analysed to distribution costs in a published income statement for a limited company?

(a) Sales director's salary

(b) Tax

(c) Depreciation of delivery vehicles

(d) Warehouse costs

3.2 Which one of the following expenses will not be analysed to administrative expenses in a published income statement for a limited company?

(a) Bank interest

(b) Office expenses

(c) General expenses

(d) Managing director's salary

3.3 Which one of the following is a non-current asset?

(a) Inventories

(b) Trade receivables

(c) Cash and cash equivalents

(d) Goodwill

3.4 Which one of the following does not appear under the heading 'Equity' in a published limited company balance sheet?

(a) Ordinary share capital

(b) Debentures

(c) Share premium account

(d) Preference shares

3.5 Which one of the following does not normally appear under the heading 'Current liabilities'?

(a) Trade payables

(b) Tax liabilities

(c) Debentures

(d) Bank overdraft

3.6 What are the responsibilities of the directors of a limited company in respect of accounting records and financial statements?

3.7   The directors of Presingold plc, a recently-formed trading company, seek your guidance on the following issues:

(a)   What items do we have to show on the face of the income statement?

(b)   How should we analyse our expenses for the income statement?

3.8   Hawksley plc is a trading company. The following information has been extracted from the books of account for the year to 31 March 20-2:

	£000
Retained earnings at 1 April 20-1	6,820
Auditors' fees	30
Tax: based on the accounting profit for the year to 31 March 20-2	1,700
Delivery expenses	1,170
Dividends paid	2,500
Non-current assets at cost:	
Delivery vans	200
Office cars	40
Warehouse premises and equipment	5,000
Non-current bank loan	1,200
Office expenses	800
Office rent, rates, electricity	350
Purchases	24,000
Revenue	35,000
Inventories at cost at 1 April 20-1	5,000
Warehouse costs	1,000
Wages and salaries:	
Delivery staff	700
Directors	300
Office staff	100
Warehouse staff	400
Bank interest	125

Additional information

1   Inventories at 31 March 20-3 are valued at cost of £6,000,000.

2   Depreciation policy

Depreciation is provided at the following annual rates on a straight-line basis: delivery vans 20%; office cars 25%; warehouse premises and equipment 10%.

3   The Directors' salaries can be split as follows:

	£000
Managing Director	120
Chairman	50
Sales Director	60
Finance Director	70

REQUIRED

Prepare for presentation to the shareholders a published income statement (including a statement of the change in retained earnings), for the year ended 31 March 20-2.

Working notes should be attached to your answer to show cost of sales, distribution costs and administrative expenses.

3.9 The following trial balance has been extracted from the books of Davidson PLC for the year ended 31 March 20-1:

	Dr £000	Cr £000
Administrative expenses	800	
Advertising expenses	50	
Authorised and issued share capital:		
ordinary shares of £1 each		1,500
Bad debts written off	20	
Cash and cash equivalents	40	
10% Debenture loan		1,000
Debenture interest (to 30 September 20-0)	50	
Trade receivables and trade payables	1,345	600
Share premium account		250
Directors' fees	400	
Distribution costs	355	
Non-current assets at cost	2,500	
accumulated depreciation (at 1 April 20-0)		500
General expenses	60	
Interim dividend paid on 1 October 20-0	75	
Purchases	4,800	
Retained earnings (at 1 April 20-0)		1,330
Rent, rates and insurance	450	
Revenue		8,500
Sales commission paid	60	
Wages and salaries paid:		
Office staff	190	
Distribution staff	285	
Inventories (at 1 April 20-0)	2,200	
	13,680	13,680

Additional information

1 Inventories at 31 March 20-1 are valued at £2,250,000.

2 The non-current assets are to be depreciated at a rate of 20% per annum on cost. The annual depreciation charge is apportioned 75% to administrative expenses and 25% to distribution costs.

3 After preparation of the trial balance, it was discovered that £50,000 was owing for rent and rates, and £100,000 had been paid in advance for insurance. Rent, rates and insurance are apportioned equally between administrative expenses and distribution costs.

4   The tax liabilities based on the profits for the year are £140,000.

5   The Directors fees can be split as follows

	£000
Chairman	70
Managing Director	125
Finance Director	105
Sales Director	100

6   The remaining debenture interest due in the year is to be accrued.

REQUIRED

Prepare the financial statements of Davidson PLC for the year ended 31 March 20-1.

3.10   The following information has been extracted from the books of Quest plc as at 30 September 20–7.

	Dr	Cr
	£000	£000
General expenses	20	
Bank overdraft		2,400
Share capital (ordinary shares of £1 each)		4,000
Share premium account		200
Delivery expenses	2,800	
Non-current assets: at cost	3,500	
Non-current assets: accumulated depreciation (at 1 October 20-6)		1,100
Investments (non-current)	2,100	
Interest received		30
Interest paid	400	
Dividends paid	80	
Office expenses	3,000	
Retained earnings (at 1 October 20-6)		840
Purchases	12,000	
Revenue		21,000
Inventories (at 1 October 20-6)	500	
Trade payables		280
Trade receivables	5,450	
	29,850	29,850

Additional information

1   Inventories at 30 September 20-7 are valued at £400,000.

2   At 30 September 20-7, £130,000 was outstanding for office expenses, and £50,000 had been paid in advance for delivery van licences.

3   Depreciation at a rate of 50% is to be charged on the cost of the non-current assets (excluding investments) using the straight-line method; it is to be apportioned as follows:

	%
Cost of sales	60
Distribution	30
Administration	10
	100

4   The tax liabilities based on the profits for the year are £80,000.

REQUIRED

Task 1

Prepare journal entries for items 1–4 listed above. Dates and narratives are not required.

Task 2

In so far as the information permits, prepare the financial statements of Quest plc for the year ended 30 September 20-7.

3.11   You have been asked to assist the directors of Lawnderer Ltd, a company that markets and distributes lawnmowers and other garden machinery, in the preparation of the financial statements for the year ended 30 September 20-5. The company employs a book-keeper who is competent in some areas of financial accounting but has gaps in his knowledge which you are required to fill. He has already prepared the extended trial balance which is shown on the next page.

The following further information is provided by the book-keeper:

1   The company disposed of motor vehicles during the year. The cost of the vehicles of £491,000 and the accumulated depreciation of £368,000 are still included in the figures in the trial balance. The sale proceeds of £187,000 were credited to the revenue account.

2   Sales commission of £52,000 relating to revenue in the year has not been paid or charged as an expense in the figures in the trial balance.

3   Interest on the 9 per cent debentures has been included in the trial balance only for the first six months of the year.

4   The tax charge for the year is £843,000.

5   The doubtful receivables provision in the trial balance has not yet been adjusted for this year. The total doubtful receivables provision required has been calculated at £115,000.

REQUIRED

Task 1

(a)   Make any adjustments you feel to be necessary to the balances in the extended trial balance as a result of the matters set out in the further information given by the book-keeper above. Set out your adjustments in the form of journal entries (narratives are not required).

(b)   Calculate the new figure for profit which would result from these adjustments being made. (Ignore any effect of these adjustments on the tax charge for the year as given above).

(c)   Show a statement of the change in retained earnings for the year.

Task 2

Prepare a balance sheet as at 30 September 20-5.

EXTENDED TRIAL BALANCE

name: Lawnderer Limited   date: 30 September 20-5

Description	Trial balance Dr £000	Trial balance Cr £000	Adjustments Dr £000	Adjustments Cr £000	Income statement Dr £000	Income statement Cr £000	Balance sheet Dr £000	Balance sheet Cr £000
Depreciation: Buildings			18		18			
Fixtures and fittings			72		72			
Motor vehicles			298		298			
Office equipment			24		24			
Accruals				102				102
Dividends paid*	120				120			
Interest on debentures	153				153			
Revenue		22,129				22,129		
Trade receivables	3,202						3,202	
Prepayments			43				43	
Bank overdraft		362						362
Cash and cash equivalents	3						3	
Purchases	14,112				14,112			
Inventories (1.10.20-4)	3,625				3,625			
Inventories (30.9.20-5)			4,572	4,572		4,572	4,572	
Retained earnings (1.10.20-4)		105						105
Provision for doubtful receivables		78						78
Trade payables		2,967						2,967
Distribution costs	4,028		37	25	4,040			
9% Debentures		3,400						3,400
Administrative expenses	1,736		65	18	1,783			
Accumulated depreciation: Buildings		83		18				101
Fixtures and fittings		214		72				286
Motor vehicles		644		298				942
Office equipment		83		24				107
Buildings (cost)	1,875						1,875	
Fixtures and fittings (cost)	576						576	
Motor vehicles (cost)	1,691						1,691	
Office equipment (cost)	244						244	
Share capital		1,000						1,000
Share premium account		300						300
Profit					2,456			2,456
	31,365	31,365	5,129	5,129	26,701	26,701	12,206	12,206

* deducted from profit

3.12 You have been asked to help prepare the financial statements of Brecked plc for the year ended 31 March 20-1. The trial balance of the company as at 31 March 20-1 is set out below.

Brecked plc
Trial balance as at 31 March 20-1

	Dr £000	Cr £000
Trade payables		2,307
Revenue		21,383
Cash and cash equivalents	185	
Interest paid	400	
Trade receivables	3,564	
Land – cost	5,150	
Buildings – cost	3,073	
Motor vehicles – cost	4,609	
Office equipment – cost	927	
Dividends paid	450	
Ordinary share capital		3,000
Accruals		135
Non-current loan		5,000
Distribution costs	2,717	
Administrative expenses	2,064	
Retained earnings at 1 April 20-0		5,340
Prepayments	92	
Share premium account		1,500
Buildings – accumulated depreciation		420
Motor vehicles – accumulated depreciation		2,014
Office equipment – accumulated depreciation		382
Inventories at 1 April 20-0	4,516	
Purchases	13,841	
Provision for doubtful receivables		107
	41,588	41,588

Additional information

- The inventories at the close of business on 31 March 20-1 are valued at cost at £5,346,000.

- The tax charge for the year is £1,473,000.

- Additions to non-current assets were:
  Motor vehicles   £1,340,000
  Office equipment   £268,000

  Motor vehicles which had cost £975,000 and which had accumulated depreciation of £506,000 were disposed of during the year. There were no other additions or disposals. All of the additions and disposals, including the relevant gain or loss on sale, have been included in the accounts as at 31 March 20-1.

- No depreciation charges for the year have been entered into the accounts as at 31 March 20-1. The depreciation charges for the year are as follows:

	£000	
Buildings	70	(to be split equally between distribution costs and administrative expenses)
Motor vehicles	648	
Office equipment	185	

- The land has been revalued by professional valuers at £6,000,000. The revaluation is to be included in the financial statements for the year ended 31 March 20-1.

REQUIRED

Task 1

Make the necessary journal entries as a result of the further information given above. Dates and narratives are not required.

Notes:

- show any workings relevant to these adjustments
- ignore any effect of these adjustments on the tax charge for the year given above

Task 2

Complete the following pro-forma to show the movement in non-current assets of Brecked plc for the year to 31 March 20-1:

NON-CURRENT ASSETS

	Land £000	Buildings £000	Motor vehicles £000	Office equipment £000
Cost at 1 April 20-0				
Revaluation				
Additions				
Disposals				
Cost/reval'n at 31 Mar 20-1				
Acc dep'n at 1 Apr 20-0				
Dep'n for year				
Disposals				
Acc Dep'n at 31 Mar 20-1				
NBV/Revaluation at 31 March 20-1				

Task 3

In so far as the information permits, prepare Brecked plc's published income statement (including a statement of the change in retained earnings) for the year to 31 March 20-1 and a balance sheet as at that date.

Note: Where relevant, working notes should be attached to your answer.

4 ACCOUNTING FOR ASSETS

4.1 Which one of the following tangible non-current assets would not normally be depreciated?

    (a)   leasehold buildings

    (b)   freehold buildings

    (c)   freehold land

    (d)   revalued leasehold land

4.2 According to IAS 38, *Intangible Assets*, which one of the following is not a criteria for capitalising development costs by a business entity?

    (a)   the entity intends to complete the intangible asset and to use or sell it

    (b)   the entity has no specific aim or application for the intangible asset

    (c)   the entity has the resources available to complete the development and to use or sell the intangible asset

    (d)   the entity has the ability to measure the development expenditure reliably

4.3 Which one of the following situations qualify as an investment property according to IAS 40, *Investment Property*?

    (a)   property held to earn rent or for capital appreciation, not being used in the ordinary course of business

    (b)   property owner occupied, being used in the ordinary course of business

    (c)   property sublet to the parent company of a group, being used in the ordinary course of business

    (d)   property sublet to a subsidiary company within the group, being used in the ordinary course of business

4.4 IAS 38, *Intangible Assets*, gives three key elements of an intangible asset. Which one of the following is not one of the three key elements?

    (a)   reliability

    (b)   identifiability

    (c)   control

    (d)   future economic benefits

4.5 To which of the following assets does IAS 36, *Impairment of Assets*, normally apply?

    1   land and buildings

    2   inventories

    3   goodwill

    4   assets held for sale

(a) all of them
(b) 1 and 2
(c) 1, 2 and 3
(d) 1 and 3

4.6 Task 1

Identify *two* external and *two* internal indicators of impairment.

Task 2

(a) Explain what is meant by an impairment review.

(b) How is an impairment review carried out?

4.7 Task 1

What are the two criteria stated by IAS 16, *Property, Plant and Equipment*, for an item of PPE to be recognised as an asset?

Task 2

IAS 16 states that, initially, PPE are measured at cost in the balance sheet.
(a) Explain what is meant by 'cost'
(b) State two attributable costs which *can be included* in the cost of an asset
(c) State two costs which *cannot be included* in the cost of an asset
(d) Briefly explain the two models from which an entity must choose as its accounting policy after acquisition of PPE

4.8 (a) Explain the two inventory valuation methods allowed by IAS 2, *Inventories*.

(b) Which method of inventory valuation cannot be used under IAS 2?

4.9 Royal Berkeley PLC owns a large number of non-current assets throughout the UK. It wishes to standardise its procedures for depreciation in accordance with IAS 16, *Property, Plant and Equipment*.

Task 1
Define depreciation.

Task 2
Outline the policy decisions Royal Berkeley PLC has to consider when accounting for IAS 16.

4.10 IAS 2, *Inventories*, states that inventories should be valued at the lower of cost and net realisable value.

Outline what is meant by the terms 'cost' and 'net realisable value'.

4.11   You have been asked to assist the directors of Lawnderer Limited, a company that markets and distributes lawnmowers and other garden machinery, in the preparation of the financial statements for the year ended 30 September 20-5.

The directors of the company have had a meeting with you regarding the possible treatment of certain future expenditure in the financial statements of the company. They have told you that the company has been approached by an inventor who has an idea to develop a revolutionary new lawnmower. The project looks technically feasible and preliminary marketing studies suggest a significant market for that product. Cost and revenue projections suggest that future profits should adequately cover the cost of development and have a beneficial effect on the future profitability of the company. The directors are concerned about the effect that the expenditure on developing the new product will have on future profits, given that it will take some time between commencing the project and commercial production.

Task

Explain how the costs of developing the new lawnmower will be reflected in the future financial statements of the company.

4.12   You have been approached by Samuel Taylor, who runs a trading company, Tayloriana Limited for help with the year end financial statements. He employs a book-keeper who has produced an extended trial balance for the company as at 31 March 20-5. Samuel is negotiating to merge his company with Coleridge Limited, which operates in the same area of activity as his own. The directors of Coleridge Limited would like to see the latest profit figures of Samuel's business. You have been asked to assist in the preparation of an income statement for the year ended 31 March 20-5.

Samuel Taylor has given you the following information from Tayloriana Limited:

1   Inventories have been counted on 31 March 20-5. The cost of the inventories calculated on a first in, first out basis is £49,300. The selling price of the inventories is estimated at £65,450.

2   After the year end, one of the trade receivables, whose year end balance was £2,500 went into liquidation. The liquidator has stated that there are no assets available to pay claimants. No provision for this bad debt has been made in the accounts and the balance is still included in year end trade receivables figure.

Task

Explain to Samuel Taylor the appropriate accounting treatment of the above items by reference to applicable accounting standards.

4.13   Prepare briefing notes for a company board meeting dealing with the following matters:

(a)   How a balance could arise on a revaluation reserve.

(b)   The recommendation of one of the directors is to lease assets as he says that this means that the assets can be kept off the balance sheet. Comment on this recommendation.

4.14   Elizabeth Ogier is the Managing Director and major shareholder of Ogier Perfumes Limited, a wholesale perfume business. She has asked you to assist in the preparation of the year end financial statements of the company.

•   The inventories at the close of business on 30 September 20-9 were valued at cost at £49,477. However, included in this balance were some items which had cost £8,200 but it is estimated that they could now be sold for only £4,800.

- The purchases figure includes items to the value of £2,000 which Elizabeth took for personal use and for gifts to friends.

Task

Draft a letter to Ms Ogier justifying any adjustments you have made to:

- the inventories valuation on 30 September 20-9

- the balances in the trial balance as a result of her taking items from the company for personal use or for gifts to friends

Your explanation should make reference, where relevant, to accounting concepts and applicable accounting standards.

5 ACCOUNTING FOR LIABILITIES AND THE INCOME STATEMENT

5.1   Tax payable in respect of the profit for the year is included in a balance sheet under:

(a)   long-term provisions

(b)   deferred taxation

(c)   non-current liabilities

(d)   current liabilities

5.2   Payments made by the lessee on an operating lease will appear:

(a)   in the income statement as an expense

(b)   in the balance sheet as a non-current asset

(c)   in the balance sheet as a non-current liability

(d)   in the income statement as revenue

5.3   According to IAS 37, *Provisions, Contingent Liabilities and Contingent Assets*, which one of the following words best describes a contingent liability?

(a)   probable

(b)   possible

(c)   remote

(d)   reliable

5.4   According to IAS 10, *Events after the Balance Sheet Date*, something that exists after the balance sheet date but has no direct link with conditions that existed at the time of the balance sheet is known as:

(a)   an adjusting event

(b)   a non-adjusting event

(c)   a contingent liability

(d)   a contingent asset

5.5   For the earnings per share calculation required by IAS 33, the amount of the profit or loss attributable to ordinary equity holders is calculated after allowing for which of the following?

1   finance costs

2   tax

3   minority interests

4   dividends on preference shares

(a)   all of them

(b)   1 and 2

(c)   2 and 3

(d)   2, 3 and 4

5.6   Under IAS 14, *Segment Reporting*, which of the following are ways in which a company must give financial information about its various activities?

1   by political segment

2   by business segment

3   by geographical segment

4   by customer segment

(a)   all of them

(b)   1 and 2

(c)   2 and 3

(d)   3 and 4

5.7   IAS 37 deals with provisions, contingent liabilities and contingent assets. What is the difference between a provision and a contingent liability?

5.8   Discuss the difference between 'earnings per share' and 'dividend per share'.

5.9   The income statement (extract) of Kingston plc for 20-8 is as follows:

Income statement (extract) for the year ended 31 December 20-8	
Continuing Operations	£000
Profit before tax	960
Tax	(210)
Profit for the year from continuing operations	750
Discontinued Operations	
Profit for the year from discontinued operations	60
Profit for the year attributable to equity holders	810

The company's share capital at 31 December 20-8 is £40m ordinary shares of £1 each. No new shares were issued during the year.

Task 1

You are asked to calculate the basic earnings per share of Kingston plc for 20-8.

Task 2

The company did consider making a new issue of £10m ordinary shares of £1 each at full market value on 1 October 20-8. Although the issue did not go ahead, the finance director asks you to calculate what the EPS figure would have been for the year.

Note: calculate EPS in pence per share, to two decimal places.

5.10   IAS 18 deals with Revenue. Explain the term 'revenue'.

5.11   You have been asked by Eliot Productions Limited to attend a board meeting of the directors at which they will approve the year end financial statements.

REQUIRED

Answer the following questions which the directors have asked about the financial statements for the year to 31 March 20-4. Justify your answers, where appropriate, by reference to accounting concepts and applicable accounting standards.

(a)   "We noted that, in preparing the accounts for the year, a trade receivables balance of £4,600 was written off as a bad debt, thus reducing profit by that amount. We understand that the customer concerned had gone into liquidation after the year end and that we did not know that the amount would not be recoverable until after 31 March 20-4. Why did we not wait until next year to write off the debt since that is when the customer went into liquidation?"

(b)   "The company is currently engaged in a legal case in which we are being sued for damages amounting to £53,000 arising out of a contract. Our lawyers are sure that we have a very good defence to the claim and, in their opinion, it is very unlikely that any damages will have to be paid. Can we ignore this claim for the purposes of our year end financial statements?"

5.12   You are employed by a firm of certified accountants and have been asked to prepare the financial statements of Franco Limited for the year to 31 March 20-5.

Task 1

You have been asked by the directors of the company to prepare some briefing notes covering the following:

Inventories are valued at the lower of cost and net realisable value in the accounts in accordance with the IAS 2. The directors would like you to explain how cost and net realisable value are derived.

Task 2

The directors of Franco Limited have drawn your attention to three matters and requested your advice on how these should be treated.

1   An issue of shares was made on 10 April 20-5. Fifty thousand ordinary shares of 50p each were issued at a premium of 25p.

2   A customer owing £30,000 to Franco Limited on 31 March 20-5 went into liquidation on 3 April 20-5. The £30,000 is still unpaid and it is unclear whether any monies will be received.

3   The company is awaiting the outcome of a legal case; an independent lawyer has assessed that it is probable that the company will gain £25,000 from it.

Write a memo to the directors of Franco Limited outlining the required treatment for each of the three events.

5.13 Following your preparation of the income statement and balance sheet of Deskover Limited, you have had a meeting with the directors at which certain other matters were raised.

One of the customers of Deskover Limited has been having cashflow problems. The account balance at the end of the year was £186,000. Against this there was a specific provision of £93,000. One month after the year end, the directors received a letter from the liquidators of the customer stating that the business had gone into liquidation. The liquidators have stated that there will be no assets available to meet any of the amounts due to the unsecured claimants.

Task

State whether any adjustments need to be made to the financial statements of Deskover Limited as a result of the liquidation of the customer. Set out any adjustment required in the form of a journal entry and justify the accounting treatment by reference to applicable accounting standards.

5.14 You have been asked to help prepare the financial statements of Brecked plc for the year ended 31 March 20-1.

Legal proceedings have been started against Brecked plc because of faulty products supplied to a customer. The company's lawyers advise that it is probable that the entity will be found liable for damages of £250,000.

REQUIRED

Task 1

Make any necessary journal entry in respect of the above information. The date and narrative are not required.

Task 2

Explain your treatment of the probable damages arising from the legal proceedings. Refer, where relevant, to accounting standards.

5.15 You have been asked to help prepare the financial statements of Leger Limited for the year ended 30 September 20-1. The trial balance of the company as at 30 September 20-1 is shown on the opposite page.

Leger Limited

Trial Balance as at 30 September 20-1

	Dr £000	Cr £000
Trade payables		1,042
Debenture interest	180	
Trade receivables	3,665	
Inventories at 1 October 20-0	3,127	
Purchases	11,581	
Interim dividend paid	300	
Share capital (ordinary shares of £1 each)		2,500
Accruals		92
9% Debenture loan		4,000
Distribution costs	3,415	
Administrative expenses	2,607	
Land – revaluation	5,637	
Buildings – cost	3,615	
Fixtures and fittings – cost	2,871	
Motor vehicles – cost	1,526	
Office equipment – cost	1,651	
Retained earnings at 1 October 20-0		6,620
Revaluation reserve		1,000
Revenue		21,324
Cash and cash equivalents	344	
Prepayments	84	
Share premium account		1,000
Buildings – accumulated depreciation		1,147
Fixtures and fittings – accumulated depreciation		963
Motor vehicles – accumulated depreciation		784
Office equipment – accumulated depreciation		214
Carriage inwards	83	
	40,686	40,686

Note: All of the operations of the company are continuing operations

Further information:

*   The inventories at the close of business on 30 September 20-1 are valued at cost at £5,408,000.

*   The tax liabilities for the year are £1,567,000.

*   Interest on the debentures has not been paid or charged in the accounts for the last six months of the year.

*   An employee was sacked on 10 October 20-1 and has now started legal proceedings for unfair dismissal. Leger Limited's lawyers consider that the company will probably lose the case and think that a reliable estimate of damages to be awarded against the company is £25,000.

*   A trade receivable with an account balance of £5,000 at 30 September 20-1 went into liquidation on 20 October 20-1. A letter from the liquidators states that there will be no assets available to meet any of the amount due to claimants.

*   Leger Limited is currently suing a competitor for copyright infringements. The case started on 22 September 20-1 and, although it has not yet concluded, Leger's lawyers consider that the company will probably win the case and be awarded damages of £50,000.

REQUIRED

Task 1

Make the necessary journal entries as a result of the further information given above. Dates and narratives are not required. (Ignore any effect of these adjustments on the tax charge for the year given above.)

Task 2

If you are not able to make any journal entries for items of further information given above, explain your reasons. Refer, where relevant, to applicable accounting standards.

Task 3

Prepare Leger Limited's income statement (including a statement of the change in retained earnings) for the year to 30 September 20-1.

Task 4

Prepare Leger Limited's balance sheet as at 30 September 20-1.

6 CASH FLOW STATEMENTS

6.1 In a cash flow statement which one of the following would appear as an inflow of cash?

(a) the gain on sale of a non-current asset

(b) a repayment of debenture loans

(c) an issue of shares at a premium

(d) an increase in inventories during the year

6.2 In a cash flow statement, which one of the following would appear as an outflow of cash?

(a) an increase in trade receivables during the year

(b) an increase in trade payables during the year

(c) depreciation charges on non-current assets

(d) the loss on sale of a non-current asset

6.3 In a cash flow statement, which one of the following is in the operating activities section?

(a) an issue of shares

(b) an issue of shares at a premium

(c) the sale of plant and equipment

(d) a decrease in inventories during the year

6.4 In a cash flow statement, which one of the following is in the financing activities section?

(a) interest paid

(b) income taxes paid

(c) purchase of non-current assets

(d) repayment of a long-term loan

6.5 The profit from operations of a business is £75,000; there were the following movements during the year:

depreciation charges	£10,000
increase in inventories	£12,000
decrease in trade receivables	£15,000
decrease in trade payables	£11,000

What is the cash from operations for the year?

(a) £73,000 inflow

(b) £123,000 inflow

(c) £27,000 inflow

(d) £77,000 inflow

6.6 In the operating activities section of a cash flow statement, gain on the sale of non-current assets is deducted because:

(a)   it is non-cash income

(b)   it is an investing activity

(c)   it is a financing activity

(d)   it is not part of a cash flow statement at all

6.7 Explain why revaluation surpluses do not appear in a cash flow statement.

6.8 Blackball PLC has made a profit from operations of £121,000 during the year ending 31 August 20-4. The income statement shows depreciation charges of £68,000 for the year and there was a profit on sale of plant and equipment amounting to £13,000. From the balance sheets for 20-4 and 20-3 the following extracted information is available:

	20-4	20-3
	£000	£000
CURRENT ASSETS		
Inventories	29	35
Trade receivables	73	57
Cash and cash equivalents	14	7
	116	99
CURRENT LIABILITIES		
Trade payables	(56)	(71)
Tax liabilities	(23)	(37)
	(79)	(108)

From the information provided, prepare a statement to show the reconciliation of profit from operations to net cash flow from operating activities for Blackball PLC for the year ended 31 August 20-4.

6.9   Set out below are financial statements for Underdesk Limited for the year ending 20-7 and also for the previous year.

Underdesk Limited
Income statement for the year ended 31 December

	20-7	20-6
	£000	£000
Revenue	5,490	4,573
Cost of sales	(3,861)	(3,201)
GROSS PROFIT	1,629	1,372
Depreciation	(672)	(445)
Other expenses	(313)	(297)
Gain on the sale of non-current assets	29	13
PROFIT FROM OPERATIONS	673	643
Interest paid	(156)	(47)
PROFIT BEFORE TAX	517	596
Tax	(129)	(124)
PROFIT AFTER TAX	388	472

Underdesk Limited
Balance sheet as at 31 December

	20-7		20-6	
	£000	£000	£000	£000
NON-CURRENT ASSETS		5,461		2,979
CURRENT ASSETS				
Inventories	607		543	
Trade receivables	481		426	
Cash and cash equivalents	–		104	
	1,088		1,073	
CURRENT LIABILITIES				
Trade payables	(371)		(340)	
Tax liabilities	(129)		(124)	
Bank overdraft	(89)		–	
	(589)		(464)	
NET CURRENT ASSETS		499		609
NON-CURRENT LIABILITIES				
Long-term loan		(1,700)		(520)
NET ASSETS		4,260		3,068
EQUITY				
Called up share capital		1,400		800
Share premium account		400		100
Retained earnings		2,460		2,168
TOTAL EQUITY		4,260		3,068

Further information

- Dividends proposed were: £96,000 in 20-6, and £180,000 in 20-7. These dividends were paid in 20-7 and 20-8 respectively.

- Non-current assets costing £187,000 with accumulated depreciation of £102,000 were sold in 20-7 for £114,000. There were no other disposals in the year.

- All revenue sales and purchases were on credit. Other expenses were paid for in cash.

REQUIRED

Task 1

Provide a reconciliation of profit from operations to net cash flow from operating activities for the year ended 31 December 20-7.

Task 2

Prepare a cash flow statement for Underdesk Limited for the year ended 31 December 20-7 in accordance with the requirements of IAS 7.

6.10 The directors have provided you with the balance sheet of Games Limited as at 30 September 20-8, along with some further information:

Games Limited

Balance sheet as at 30 September

	20-8	20-7
	£000	£000
NON-CURRENT ASSETS	1,845	1,615
CURRENT ASSETS		
Inventories	918	873
Trade receivables	751	607
Cash and cash equivalents	23	87
	1,692	1,567
CURRENT LIABILITIES		
Trade payables	(583)	(512)
Tax liabilities	(62)	(54)
	(645)	(566)
NET CURRENT ASSETS	1,047	1,001
NON-CURRENT LIABILITIES		
Long-term loan	(560)	(420)
NET ASSETS	2,332	2,196
EQUITY		
Called up share capital	1,000	1,000
Share premium account	100	100
Retained earnings	1,232	1,096
TOTAL EQUITY	2,332	2,196

Further information

- No non-current assets were sold during the year. The depreciation charge for the year amounted to £277,000.

- All revenue sales and purchases were on credit. Other expenses were paid for in cash.

- The profit after tax was £184,000. Interest of £56,000 was paid in the year. Tax was £62,000 for the year.

REQUIRED

Provide a reconciliation of profit from operations to net cash flow from operating activities for Games Limited for the year ended 30 September 20-8.

Note:

You are not required to prepare a cash flow statement.

6.11 A colleague has asked you to take over the drafting of a cash flow statement for Diewelt Limited for the year ended 30 September 20-9. Your colleague has already drafted the figure for cash from operations. The financial statements of the company, drafted for internal purposes, along with the calculation of cash from operations are set out below with some further information relating to the reporting year:

Diewelt Limited

Income statement for the year ended 30 September 20-9

	20-9
	£000
Revenue	9,804
Cost of sales	(5,784)
GROSS PROFIT	4,020
Gain on sale of non-current assets	57
Depreciation	(985)
Other expenses	(819)
PROFIT FROM OPERATIONS	2,273
Interest paid	(365)
PROFIT BEFORE TAX	1,908
Tax	(583)
PROFIT AFTER TAX	1,325

Diewelt Limited

Balance sheet as at 30 September

	20-9		20-8	
	£000	£000	£000	£000
NON-CURRENT ASSETS		6,490		5,620
CURRENT ASSETS				
Inventories	3,151		2,106	
Trade receivables	2,314		1,470	
Cash and cash equivalents	103		383	
	5,568		3,959	
CURRENT LIABILITIES				
Trade payables	(964)		(1,034)	
Tax liabilities	(583)		(491)	
	(1,547)		(1,525)	
NET CURRENT ASSETS		4,021		2,434
NON-CURRENT LIABILITIES				
Long-term loan		(3,300)		(2,900)
NET ASSETS		7,211		5,154
EQUITY				
Called up share capital		2,200		1,600
Share premium account		800		300
Retained earnings		4,211		3,254
TOTAL EQUITY		7,211		5,154

Further information

- Dividends proposed were: £368,000 in 20-8 and £484,000 in 20-9. These dividends were paid in 20-9 and 20-0 respectively.

- A non-current asset which had cost £136,000 and had accumulated depreciation of £85,000 was sold during the year.

- All revenue sales and purchases were on credit. Other expenses were paid for in cash.

Calculation of cash from operations

	£000
Profit from operations	2,273
Depreciation charges	985
Gain on sale of non-current assets	(57)
Increase in inventories	(1,045)
Increase in trade receivables	(844)
Decrease in trade payables	(70)
Cash from operations	1,242

REQUIRED

Prepare a cash flow statement for Diewelt Limited for the year ended 30 September 20-9 in accordance with the requirements of IAS 7. The statement should start with the figure for cash from operations of £1,242,000 (see above).

6.12 Kasper PLC's income statement for the year to 31 December 20-3 and balance sheets for 20-2 and 20-3 were as follows:

Kasper PLC: Income statement for the year to 31 December 20-3.

	£000	£000
Revenue		820
Materials	166	
Wages and salaries	98	
Depreciation charges	118	
Loss on sale of non-current asset	18	(400)
PROFIT FROM OPERATIONS		420
Interest paid		(30)
PROFIT BEFORE TAX		390
Tax		(130)
PROFIT AFTER TAX		260

Kasper PLC: Balance sheet as at 31 December

	20-3		20-2	
NON-CURRENT ASSETS	£000	£000	£000	£000
At cost	1,596		1,560	
Depreciation	(318)	1,278	(224)	1,336
CURRENT ASSETS				
Inventories	24		20	
Trade receivables	66		50	
Cash and cash equivalents	58		64	
	148		134	
CURRENT LIABILITIES				
Trade payables	(12)		(6)	
Tax liabilities	(102)		(86)	
	(114)		(92)	
NET CURRENT ASSETS		34		42
		1,312		1,378
NON-CURRENT LIABILITIES				
Loans and debentures		(200)		(500)
NET ASSETS		1,112		878
EQUITY				
Called up share capital		360		340
Share premium account		36		24
Retained earnings		716		514
TOTAL EQUITY		1,112		878

Note to the accounts

- During the year the company paid £90,000 for a new piece of machinery.

REQUIRED

Prepare a reconciliation of profit from operations to net cash flow from operating activities for Kasper PLC for the year ended 31 December 20-3.

Note: You are not required to prepare the actual cash flow statement.

6.13 Hill PLC's income statement for the year to 31 December 20-3 and balance sheets for 20-2 and 20-3 were as follows:

Hill PLC: abridged Income statement for the year to 31 December 20-3.

	£
PROFIT FROM OPERATIONS	57,500
Interest received	2,500
Interest paid	(4,000)
PROFIT BEFORE TAX	56,000
Tax	(20,000)
PROFIT FOR THE YEAR	36,000

Hill PLC: Balance sheet as at 31 December

	20-2		20-3	
NON-CURRENT ASSETS	£000	£000	£000	£000
Property at cost	260		280	
Depreciation to date	(60)	200	(68)	212
Plant & Equipment at cost	164		200	
Depreciation to date	(54)	110	(86)	114
		310		326
CURRENT ASSETS				
Inventories	56		72	
Trade receivables	52		48	
Short-term bank deposit	16		20	
Cash at bank	14		30	
	138		170	
CURRENT LIABILITIES				
Trade payables	(40)		(54)	
Tax liabilities	(32)		(24)	
	(72)		(78)	
NET CURRENT ASSETS		66		92
		376		418
NON-CURRENT LIABILITIES				
10% Debentures		(80)		(20)
NET ASSETS		296		398
EQUITY				
Called up share capital		200		260
Share premium account		24		56
Retained earnings		72		82
TOTAL EQUITY		296		398

Notes to the accounts

• Dividends proposed were: £26,000 in 20-2 and £35,000 in 20-3. These dividends were paid in 20-3 and 20-4 respectively.

• There were no sales of property during the year.

• During the year the company sold plant costing £38,000 on which there was accumulated depreciation totalling £8,000. The net proceeds from the sale amounted to £24,000.

REQUIRED

(a) Prepare a cash flow statement for Hill PLC for the year to 31 December 20-3 in accordance with IAS 7.

(b) Identify *two* main sources of cash of Hill PLC shown by the cash flow statement.

6.14 You have been asked to assist in the calculation of the net cash from operating activities for Poised Limited for the year ended 31 July 20-6. The financial statements of the company drafted for internal purposes are set out below, along with some further information relating to the reporting year.

Poised Limited

Income statement for the year ended 31 July 20-6

		20-6
		£000
Revenue		12,482
Opening inventories	2,138	
Purchases	8,530	
Less Closing inventories	2,473	
Cost of sales		(8,195)
GROSS PROFIT		4,287
Depreciation		(1,347)
Other expenses		(841)
PROFIT FROM OPERATIONS		2,099
Interest paid		(392)
PROFIT BEFORE TAX		1,707
Tax		(562)
PROFIT FOR THE YEAR		1,145

Poised Limited

Balance sheet as at 31 July

	20-6	20-5
	£000	£000
NON-CURRENT ASSETS	6,867	6,739
CURRENT ASSETS		
Inventories	2,473	2,138
Trade receivables	1,872	1,653
Cash and cash equivalents	1,853	149
	6,198	3,940
CURRENT LIABILITIES		
Trade payables	(1,579)	(1,238)
Tax liabilities	(562)	(477)
	(2,141)	(1,715)
NET CURRENT ASSETS	4,057	2,225
NON-CURRENT LIABILITIES		
Long-term loan	(4,200)	(3,800)
NET ASSETS	6,724	5,164
EQUITY		
Called up share capital	3,000	2,500
Share premium account	400	100
Retained earnings	3,324	2,564
TOTAL EQUITY	6,724	5,164

Further information

1   No fixed assets were sold during the year.

2   All revenue sales and purchases were on credit. Other expenses were paid for in cash.

REQUIRED

Provide a reconciliation of profit from operations to net cash flow from operating activities for Poised Limited for the year ended 31 July 20-6.

Note: You are NOT required to prepare the remainder of the cash flow statement.

6.15 You have been asked to prepare a calculation of the net cash from operating activities for Sholti Limited for the year ended 31 March 20-2. The income statement and balance sheets of Sholti Limited are set out below.

Sholti Limited
Income statement for the year ended 31 March 20-2

	£000
Revenue	32,347
Cost of sales	(14,243)
GROSS PROFIT	18,104
Gain on the sale of non-current assets	378
Distribution costs	(6,157)
Administrative expenses	(4,892)
PROFIT FROM OPERATIONS	7,433
Interest paid	(625)
PROFIT BEFORE TAX	6,808
Tax	(1,967)
PROFIT FOR THE YEAR	4,841

Sholti Limited
Balance sheet as at 31 March

	20-2		20-1	
	£000	£000	£000	£000
NON-CURRENT ASSETS		22,972		10,080
CURRENT ASSETS				
Inventories	8,632		9,013	
Trade receivables	5,391		4,728	
Cash and cash equivalents	–		987	
	14,023		14,728	
CURRENT LIABILITIES				
Trade payables	(2,382)		(2,081)	
Tax liabilities	(1,967)		(1,522)	
	(4,349)		(3,603)	
NET CURRENT ASSETS		9,674		11,125
NON-CURRENT LIABILITIES				
Long-term loan		(8,000)		(6,000)
NET ASSETS		24,646		15,205
EQUITY				
Called up share capital		12,000		8,000
Share premium account		4,000		2,000
Retained earnings		8,646		5,205
TOTAL EQUITY		24,646		15,205

Further information

- The total depreciation charge for the year was £1,850,000.

- All revenue sales and purchases were on credit. Other expenses were paid for in cash.

REQUIRED

Prepare a reconciliation of profit from operations to net cash flow from operating activities for Sholti Limited for the year ended 31 March 20-2.

Note: You are NOT required to prepare the remainder of the cash flow statement.

7 INTERPRETATION OF FINANCIAL STATEMENTS

7.1 For the ratio return on capital employed, which one of the following best describes capital employed?

(a)   share capital

(b)   share capital + reserves

(c)   share capital + reserves + non-current liabilities

(d)   share capital + reserves + non-current liabilities + current liabilities

7.2 Which one of the following best describes the acid test or quick ratio?

(a)   current assets : current liabilities

(b)   trade receivables : trade payables

(c)   (current assets – inventories) : current liabilities

(d)   current assets : (current liabilities – bank overdraft)

7.3 For the asset turnover ratio, which one of the following best describes net assets?

(a)   non-current assets + current assets

(b)   non-current assets + current assets – current liabilities

(c)   current assets – current liabilities

(d)   non-current assets + current assets – current liabilities – non-current liabilities

7.4 The following information was extracted from the income statement of Blue Dawn PLC for the year ending 31 December 20-7:

	£000
Profit from operations	1,200
Interest paid	(200)
Profit before tax	1,000
Tax	(150)
Profit after tax	850

What is the interest cover for the business?

(a)   8 times

(b)   6 times

(c)   5 times

(d)   1.2 times

7.5   The following information was extracted from the financial statements of Jacob PLC for the year 30 September 20-3

	£000
Revenue	10,000
Purchases	4,000
Trade receivables	2,000
Trade payables	1,000

What is the payables payment period (to the nearest day)?

(a)   37 days

(b)   73 days

(c)   16 days

(d)   91 days

7.6   The following information was extracted from the balance sheet of Aktar PLC as at 31 July 20-5

	£000
10% Debentures	3,000
Ordinary shares of £1 each	5,000
7% Preference shares of 50p each	2,000
Share premium account	2,000
Retained earnings	8,000

What is the gearing ratio (debt/equity) for the company?

(a)   20%

(b)   40%

(c)   33%

(d)   35%

7.7   Identify four user groups who would be interested in examining the financial ratios of a company.

7.8   Explain why the gearing and interest cover ratios are relevant to a investor who wishes to purchase ordinary shares in a company.

7.9   Jonathan Fisher is intending to invest a substantial sum of money in a company. A colleague has suggested to him that he might want to invest in a private company called Carp Ltd which supplies the pond equipment to retail outlets. You have been asked to assist him in interpreting the financial statements of the company which are set out below:

Carp Ltd

Summary Income statements for the year ended 30 September

	20-9	20-8
	£000	£000
Revenue	3,183	2,756
Cost of sales	(1,337)	(1,020)
GROSS PROFIT	1,846	1,736
Expenses	(1,178)	(1,047)
PROFIT FROM OPERATIONS	668	689
Finance costs	(225)	(92)
PROFIT BEFORE TAX	443	597
Tax	(87)	(126)
PROFIT FOR THE YEAR	356	471

Carp Ltd

Summary Balance sheets as at 30 September

	20-9		20-8	
	£000	£000	£000	£000
NON-CURRENT ASSETS		4,214		2,030
CURRENT ASSETS				
Inventories	795		689	
Trade receivables	531		459	
Cash and cash equivalents	15		136	
	1,341		1,284	
CURRENT LIABILITIES				
Trade payables	(751)		(485)	
Tax liabilities	(87)		(126)	
	(838)		(611)	
NET CURRENT ASSETS		503		673
NON-CURRENT LIABILITIES				
Long-term loan		(2,500)		(1,000)
		2,217		1,703
EQUITY				
Share capital		700		500
Retained earnings		1,517		1,203
TOTAL EQUITY		2,217		1,703

REQUIRED

Prepare notes for Jonathan Fisher covering the following points:

1   Calculate the following ratios for the two years:
    (a)   gearing
    (b)   net profit percentage
    (c)   current ratio
    (d)   return on equity

2   Using the ratios calculated, comment on the company's profitability, liquidity and financial position and consider how these have changed over the two years.

3   Using only the calculation of the ratios and the analysis of the changes over the two years, state whether the company is a better prospect for investment in 20-9 than it was in 20-8. Give reasons for your answers.

7.10 A director of the company where you work is going to a conference where one of the topics to be discussed is gearing. He has asked you to prepare a briefing paper containing the following points:
- What do you understand by the term gearing?
- What effect can gearing have on a company's profit and how will gearing affect the overall return to the ordinary shareholder?

If possible you should supply a worked example to back up your answer.

7.11 Botticelli Limited is a trading company that sells carpets to retail outlets. The shareholders of Botticelli Limited have some questions about the profitability and liquidity of the company and about how cash flows from operating activities can be reconciled to operating profit. The income statement and balance sheet produced for internal purposes are set out below:

Botticelli Limited

Income statement for the year ended 31 December

	20-6		20-5	
	£000	*£000*	*£000*	*£000*
Revenue		2,963		1,736
Opening inventories	341		201	
Purchases	1,712		1,097	
Less Closing inventories	419		341	
Cost of sales		(1,634)		(957)
GROSS PROFIT		1,329		779
Depreciation		(247)		(103)
Other expenses		(588)		(334)
Gain on sale of non-current assets		15		–
PROFIT FROM OPERATIONS		509		342
Finance costs		(78)		(26)
PROFIT BEFORE TAX		431		316
Tax		(138)		(111)
PROFIT FOR THE YEAR		293		205

Botticelli Limited

Balance sheet as at 31 December

	20-6	20-5
	£000	£000
NON-CURRENT ASSETS	2,800	1,013
CURRENT ASSETS		
Inventories	419	341
Trade receivables	444	381
Cash and cash equivalents	–	202
	863	924
CURRENT LIABILITIES		
Trade payables	(370)	(238)
Tax liabilities	(158)	(103)
Bank overdraft	(194)	–
	(722)	(341)
NET CURRENT ASSETS	141	583
NON-CURRENT LIABILITIES		
Long-term loan	(970)	(320)
	1,971	1,276
EQUITY		
Called up share capital	400	200
Share premium account	250	–
Retained earnings	1,321	1,076
TOTAL EQUITY	1,971	1,276

REQUIRED

Prepare a report to the shareholders about the profitability and liquidity of Botticelli Ltd for the two years 20-5 and 20-6. Your report should include:

(a)   calculation of the following ratios for the two years:

– return on capital employed

– gross profit ratio

– net profit ratio

– current ratio

– quick ratio (also called acid test)

(b)   comments on the changes in the ratios from 20-5 to 20-6.

7.12 Due to the success of its board game 'The Absolute', McTaggart Limited is thinking of expanding its operations. It has identified another company, Hegel Limited, which also distributes board games, as a possible target for takeover. The directors have obtained a set of financial statements of the company for the last two years; these have been prepared for internal purposes. Hegel Limited's year end is 30 September.

The directors have a number of questions relating to the company and to the possible takeover which they would like you to answer. The financial statements for Hegel Limited are set out below:

Hegel Limited

Income statement for the year ended 30 September

	20-7		20-6	
	£000	£000	£000	£000
Revenue		6,995		3,853
Opening inventories	681		432	
Purchases	4,245		2,561	
Less Closing inventories	729		681	
Cost of sales		(4,197)		(2,312)
GROSS PROFIT		2,798		1,541
Depreciation		(971)		(311)
Other expenses		(593)		(415)
Gain on sale of non-current assets		20		–
PROFIT FROM OPERATIONS		1,254		815
Finance costs		(302)		(28)
PROFIT BEFORE TAX		952		787
Tax		(333)		(276)
PROFIT FOR THE YEAR		619		511

Hegel Limited

Balance sheet as at 30 September

	20-7	20-6
	£000	£000
NON-CURRENT ASSETS	6,472	2,075
CURRENT ASSETS		
Inventories	729	681
Trade receivables	574	469
Cash and cash equivalents	–	320
	1,303	1,470
CURRENT LIABILITIES		
Trade payables	(484)	(544)
Tax liabilities	(333)	(276)
Bank overdraft	(158)	–
	(975)	(820)
NET CURRENT ASSETS	328	650
NON-CURRENT LIABILITIES		
Long-term loan	(3,350)	(350)
	3,450	2,375
EQUITY		
Called up share capital	1,200	1,000
Share premium account	400	–
Retained earnings	1,850	1,375
TOTAL EQUITY	3,450	2,375

Further information

All revenue sales and purchases were on credit. Other expenses were paid for in cash.

REQUIRED

Prepare a report for the directors of McTaggart Limited which covers the relevant calculations and questions set out below:

(a)   Calculate the current and quick ratios (also known as the 'acid test') of Hegel Limited for the two years. Using this information state how the liquidity of Hegel Limited has changed from 20-6 to 20-7.

(b)   Calculate the gearing ratio for Hegel Limited for 20-6 and 20-7 and comment on the results. Explain whether the level of borrowings in Hegel Limited would have any impact on the level of gearing in the group accounts of McTaggart Limited.

7.13   Duncan Tweedy wishes to invest some money in one of two private companies. He has obtained the latest financial statements for Byrne Limited and May Limited prepared for internal purposes. As part of his decision-making process he has asked you to assess the relative profitability of the two companies. The financial statements of the companies are set out as follows.

Summary income statement

for the year ended 30th September

	Byrne Ltd	May Ltd
	£000	£000
Revenue	5,761	2,927
Cost of sales	(2,362)	(966)
GROSS PROFIT	3,399	1,961
Distribution costs	(922)	(468)
Administrative expenses	(1,037)	(439)
PROFIT FROM OPERATIONS	1,440	1,054
Finance costs	(152)	(40)
PROFIT BEFORE TAX	1,288	1,014
Tax	(309)	(243)
PROFIT FOR THE YEAR	979	771

Balance sheet as at 30 September 20-1

	Byrne Ltd		May Ltd	
	£000	£000	£000	£000
NON-CURRENT ASSETS		6,188		2,725
CURRENT ASSETS	1,522		1,102	
CURRENT LIABILITIES	(1,015)		(545)	
NET CURRENT ASSETS		507		557
NON-CURRENT LIABILITIES				
Long-term loan		(1,900)		(500)
		4,795		2,782
EQUITY				
Called up share capital: ordinary shares of £1 each		2,083		939
Retained earnings		2,712		1,843
TOTAL EQUITY		4,795		2,782

You have also been given the following ratios:

	Byrne Ltd	May Ltd
Return on capital employed	21.5%	32.1%
Gross profit percentage	59.0%	67.0%
Net profit percentage (using profit from operations)	25.0%	36.0%
Earnings per share	47p	82p

REQUIRED

Prepare a report for Duncan Tweedy that:

(a) explains the meaning of each ratio

(b) uses each ratio to comment on the relative profitability of the companies

(c) concludes – with reasons – which of the two companies is the more profitable

7.14 Page Limited is a company that supplies stationery for business and domestic purposes. You have been asked to assist the directors in the interpretation of the financial statements of the company. They are intending to apply to the bank for a substantial loan. The bank has asked them for their financial statements for the last two years. The directors wish to know how the bank will view their profitability, liquidity and financial position on the evidence of these financial statements.

The directors are also concerned that they do not fully understand the financial statements of customers to whom they supply stationery. The customers include public sector and other not-for-profit organisations.

You have been supplied with the income statement and the balance sheet of Page Limited for two years, prepared for internal purposes.

Page Limited

Income statement for the year ended 31 March

	20-9	20-8
	£000	£000
Revenue	2,636	1,687
Cost of sales	(923)	(590)
GROSS PROFIT	1,713	1,097
Depreciation	(856)	(475)
Other expenses	(126)	(101)
Gain on sale of non-current assets	7	2
PROFIT FROM OPERATIONS	738	523
Finance costs	(252)	(120)
PROFIT BEFORE TAX	486	403
Tax	(165)	(137)
PROFIT FOR THE YEAR	321	266

Page Limited
Balance sheet as at 31 March

	20-9	20-8
	£000	£000
NON-CURRENT ASSETS	4,282	2,376
CURRENT ASSETS		
Inventories	448	287
Trade receivables	527	337
Cash and cash equivalents	–	86
	975	710
CURRENT LIABILITIES		
Trade payables	(401)	(222)
Tax liabilities	(165)	(137)
Bank overdraft	(183)	–
	(749)	(359)
NET CURRENT ASSETS	226	351
NON-CURRENT LIABILITIES		
Long-term loan	(2,800)	(1,500)
	1,708	1,227
EQUITY		
Called up share capital	200	100
Share premium account	100	–
Retained earnings	1,408	1,127
TOTAL EQUITY	1,708	1,227

REQUIRED

Prepare a report for the directors which includes the following:

(a)   a calculation of the following ratios of Page Limited for the two years:

(i)   Return on equity
(ii)   Net profit percentage
(iii)   Quick ratio/acid test
(iv)   Gearing ratio
(v)   Interest cover

(b)   comments on the profitability, liquidity and the financial position of the company as revealed by the ratios and a statement of how this has changed over the two years covered by the financial statements

(c)   an opinion as to whether the bank would be likely to give the company a substantial loan based solely on the information in the financial statements

8 CONSOLIDATED ACCOUNTS

8.1 Active PLC invested £220,000 in 120,000 ordinary shares of 50 pence each of Doldrums PLC. The issued share capital and reserves of Doldrums PLC at the time of acquisition were £80,000 in shares and £60,000 in reserves (£140,000 in total).

What is the value of goodwill arising on acquisition?

(a) £80,000

(b) £115,000

(c) £55,000

(d) £140,000

8.2 The issued share capital of Sub Let PLC is 800,000 ordinary shares of 10 pence each. The reserves are: share premium account £40,000, revaluation reserve £25,000 and retained earnings £85,000. The parent company Ask Right PLC currently owns 500,000 of the ordinary shares in Sub Let PLC.

What is the total value for minority interest?

(a) £86,250

(b) £356,250

(c) £300,000

(d) £143,750

8.3 The balance sheet of Father PLC includes trade receivables of £65,000 and its subsidiary company Son Limited has trade receivables totalling £32,000. The accounts also show trade payables to be £52,000 and £18,000 respectively. However included in these amounts are inter-group balances of £7,000 (Father PLC owes Son Limited).

In the consolidated balance sheet of the group what will be the respective trade receivables and trade payables figures?

(a) £97,000 and £70,000

(b) £104,000 and £77,000

(c) £90,000 and £63,000

(d) £33,000 and £34,000

8.4 Mother PLC acquires 80% of the ordinary shares in Daughter Limited, on 1 April 20-7. The profit for the year after tax reported by Daughter Limited for the year ended 31 March 20-8 amounted to £65,000.

What is the minority interest that will appear in the consolidated income statement for the year ended 31 March 20-8?

(a) £52,000

(b) £65,000

(c) £26,000

(d) £13,000

8.5 Duck PLC owns 55% of the ordinary shares in Duckling Limited. Revenue for the year for Duck PLC amounted to £800,000 whereas Duckling Limited had revenue of £350,000. Duckling Limited's revenue includes goods sold to Duck PLC for £16,000. These goods as yet have not been resold by Duck PLC to any customer.

What is the correct value for revenue which will appear in the consolidated income statement?

(a) £1,150,000

(b) £992,500

(c) £1,118,000

(d) £1,134,000

8.6 What is the correct term used for a subsidiary company's reserves at the time of acquisition by a parent company?

(a) pre-acquisition profit

(b) post-acquisition profit

(c) takeover profit

(d) minority interest

8.7 IFRS 3, *Business Combinations*, identifies a number of features in the preparation of consolidated accounts. Explain the following:
- method of accounting to be used in acquisitions
- assets and liabilities acquired
- goodwill

8.8 (a) In business combinations, how are fair values to be treated on acquisition?

(b) What effect do fair values have on the calculations for:
- goodwill
- minority interest
- post-acquisition profits

8.9 An investment figure of £4,010,000 shown in the financial statements of Deskover Limited represents the cost of acquiring shares in a subsidiary undertaking, Underdesk Limited. Deskover Limited acquired 75% of the ordinary share capital of Underdesk Limited on 31 December 20-7. The directors have obtained a balance sheet of the company for the last two years, prepared for internal purposes. Underdesk Limited 's year end is also 31 December. The net assets of Underdesk Limited are shown in the balance sheet at their fair values except for the non-current assets, which have a fair value at 31 December 20-7 of £5,761,000.

Underdesk Limited

Balance sheet as at 31 December

	20-7		20-6	
	£000	£000	£000	£000
NON-CURRENT ASSETS		5,461		2,979
CURRENT ASSETS				
Inventories	607		543	
Trade receivables	481		426	
Cash and cash equivalents	–		104	
	1,088		1,073	
CURRENT LIABILITIES				
Trade payables	(551)		(436)	
Tax liabilities	(129)		(124)	
Bank overdraft	(89)		–	
	(769)		(560)	
NET CURRENT ASSETS		319		513
NON-CURRENT LIABILITIES				
Long-term loan		(1,700)		(520)
NET ASSETS		4,080		2,972
EQUITY				
Called up share capital		1,400		800
Share premium account		400		100
Retained earnings		2,280		2,072
TOTAL EQUITY		4,080		2,972

REQUIRED

Calculate the goodwill on consolidation that arose on acquisition of the shares in Underdesk Limited on 31 December 20-7. Set out the accounting treatment of this goodwill in the group accounts of Deskover Limited, justifying your answer by reference to applicable accounting standards.

Note: You are not required to produce a consolidated balance sheet for the group.

8.10 The directors of Fun Limited have a number of questions relating to the financial statements of their recently acquired subsidiary, Games Limited. Fun Limited acquired 75% of the ordinary share capital of Games Limited on 30 September 20-8 for £2,244,000. The fair value of the non-current assets in Games Limited as at 30 September 20-8 was £2,045,000. The directors have provided you with the balance sheet of Games Limited as at 30 September 20-8 along with some further information:

Games Limited

Balance sheet as at 30 September

	20-8	20-7
	£000	£000
NON-CURRENT ASSETS	1,845	1,615
CURRENT ASSETS		
Inventories	918	873
Trade receivables	751	607
Cash and cash equivalents	23	87
	1,692	1,567
CURRENT LIABILITIES		
Trade payables	(635)	(560)
Tax liabilities	(62)	(54)
	(697)	(614)
NET CURRENT ASSETS	995	953
NON-CURRENT LIABILITIES		
Long-term loan	(560)	(420)
NET ASSETS	2,280	2,148
EQUITY		
Called up share capital	1,000	1,000
Share premium account	100	100
Retained earnings	1,180	1,048
TOTAL EQUITY	2,280	2,148

REQUIRED

Prepare notes to take to the Board meeting to answer the following questions of the directors:

(a)   What figure for the minority interest would appear in the consolidated balance sheet of Fun Limited as at 30 September 20-8?

(b)   Where in the balance sheet would the minority interest be disclosed?

(c)   What is a 'minority interest'?

8.11 Fertwrangler Limited has one subsidiary undertaking, Voncarryon Limited, which it acquired on 1 April 20-1. The balance sheet of Voncarryon Limited as at 31 March 20-2 is set out below.

Voncarryon Limited

Balance sheet as at 31 March 2002

	£000	£000
Non-current assets		3,855
Current assets	4,961	
Current liabilities	(2,546)	
Net current assets		2,415
Non-current (long-term) loan		(1,500)
Net assets		4,770
Equity		
Called up share capital		2,000
Share premium account		1,000
Retained earnings		1,770
Total equity		4,770

Further information:

- The share capital of Voncarryon Limited consists of ordinary shares of £1 each. There have been no changes to the balances of share capital and share premium during the year. No dividends were paid by Voncarryon Limited during the year.

- Fertwrangler Limited acquired 1,200,000 shares in Voncarryon Limited on 1 April 20-1 at a cost of £3,510,000.

- At 1 April 20-1 the balance of retained earnings of Voncarryon Limited was £1,350,000.

- The fair value of the non-current assets of Voncarryon Limited at 1 April 20-1 was £4,455,000. The book value of the non-current assets at 1 April 20-1 was £4,055,000. The revaluation has not been reflected in the books of Voncarryon Limited.

- Ten per cent of the goodwill arising on consolidation is to be written off as an impairment loss in the year to 31 March 20-2.

REQUIRED

Calculate the goodwill figure relating to the acquisition of Voncarryon Limited that will appear in the consolidated balance sheet of Fertwrangler Limited as at 31 March 20-2.

8.12 You have been asked to assist in the preparation of the consolidated accounts of the Bloomsbury Group. Set out on the next page are the balance sheets of Woolf Limited and Forster Limited for the year ended 31 March 20-1:

Balance Sheets as at 31 March 20-1

	Woolf Limited		Forster Limited	
	£000	£000	£000	£000
Tangible non-current assets		12,995		1,755
Investment in Forster Limited		1,978		–
Current assets				
Inventories	3,586		512	
Trade receivables	2,193		382	
Cash and cash equivalents	84		104	
	5,863		998	
Current liabilities				
Trade payables	(2,080)		(273)	
Tax liabilities	(667)		(196)	
	(2,747)		(469)	
Net current assets		3,116		529
Non-current (long-term) loan		–		(400)
Net assets		18,089		1,884
Equity				
Share capital		2,000		1,000
Share premium account		–		200
Retained earnings		16,089		684
Total equity		18,089		1,884

Further information:

- The share capital of both Woolf Limited and Forster Limited consists of ordinary shares of £1 each. There have been no changes to the balances of share capital and share premium during the year. No dividends were paid by Forster Limited during the year.

- Woolf Limited acquired 750,000 shares in Forster Limited on 31 March 20-0.

- At 31 March 20-0 the balance of retained earnings of Forster Limited was £424,000.

- The fair value of the non-current assets of Forster Limited at 31 March 20-0 was £2,047,000 as compared with their book value of £1,647,000. The revaluation has not been reflected in the books of Forster Limited. (Ignore any depreciation implications).

- Ten per cent of the goodwill arising on consolidation is to be written off as an impairment loss in the year to 31 March 20-1.

REQUIRED

Prepare the consolidated balance sheet of Woolf Limited and its subsidiary undertaking as at 31 March 20–1.

8.13 You have been asked to assist in the preparation of the consolidated accounts of the Shopan Group. Set out below are the balance sheets of Shopan Limited and its subsidiary undertaking Hower Limited, as at 30 September 20-9:

Balance sheets as at 30 September 20-9

	Shopan Limited		Hower Limited	
	£000	£000	£000	£000
Tangible non-current assets		6,273		1,633
Investment in Hower Limited		2,100		
Current assets				
Inventories	1,901		865	
Trade receivables	1,555		547	
Cash and cash equivalents	184		104	
	3,640		1,516	
Current liabilities				
Trade payables	(1,516)		(457)	
Tax liabilities	(431)		(188)	
	(1,947)		(645)	
Net current assets		1,693		871
Non-current (long-term) loan		(2,870)		(400)
Net assets		7,196		2,104
Equity				
Called up share capital		2,000		500
Share premium account		950		120
Retained earnings		4,246		1,484
Total equity		7,196		2,104

Further information

- The share capital of both Shopan Limited and Hower Limited consists of ordinary shares of £1 each.
- Shopan Limited acquired 375,000 shares in Hower Limited on 30 September 20-9.
- The fair value of the non-current assets of Hower Limited at 30 September 20-9 was £2,033,000.

REQUIRED

Task 1

Prepare the consolidated balance sheet for Shopan Limited and its subsidiary undertaking as at 30 September 20-9.

Task 2

IFRS 3, *Business Combinations*, defines control over another business as 'the power to govern the financial and operating policies of an entity or business so as to obtain benefits from its activities'. Give two of the criteria that, according to IFRS 3, give control of an entity.

8.14 The Finance Director of Fairway plc has asked you to prepare the draft consolidated income statement for the group. The company has one subsidiary, Green Limited. The income statements of the two companies, prepared for internal purposes, for the year ended 30 June 20-2 are as follows:

	Fairway plc	*Green Limited*
Continuing Operations	*£000*	*£000*
Revenue	12,200	4,400
Cost of sales	(8,500)	(3,100)
Gross profit	3,700	1,300
Distribution costs	(1,600)	(500)
Administrative expenses	(400)	(200)
Dividends received from Green Limited	80	–
Profit from operations	1,780	600
Finance costs	(300)	(200)
Profit before tax	1,480	400
Tax	(400)	(100)
Profit for the year	1,080	300

Further information:

- Fairway plc acquired 80% of the ordinary share capital of Green Limited on 1 July 20-1.

- During the year Green Limited sold goods which had cost £750,000 to Fairway plc for £1,000,000. All the goods had been sold by Fairway plc by the end of the year.

- Dividends paid during the year were:
     Fairway plc, £700,000
     Green Limited, £100,000

- There were no impairment losses on goodwill during the year.

REQUIRED

Draft a consolidated income statement for Fairway plc and its subsidiary undertaking for the year ended 30 June 20-2.

8.15 The Finance Director of Wood plc has asked you to prepare the draft consolidated income statement for the group. The company has one subsidiary undertaking, Plank Limited. The income statements for the two companies, prepared for internal purposes, for the year ended 31 March 20–1 are set out below.

Income statements for the year ended 31 March 20-1

	Wood plc	Plank Limited
Continuing Operations	£000	£000
Revenue	31,600	10,800
Cost of sales	(17,000)	(5,600)
Gross profit	14,600	5,200
Distribution costs	(3,600)	(1,300)
Administrative expenses	(3,000)	(1,160)
Dividends received from Plank Limited	600	
Profit from operations	8,600	2,740
Finance costs	(1,600)	(240)
Profit before tax	7,000	2,500
Tax	(2,240)	(740)
Profit for the year	4,760	1,760

Further information:

- Wood plc acquired 75% of the ordinary share capital of Plank Limited on 1 April 20-0.

- During the year Plank Limited sold goods which had cost £600,000 to Wood plc for £1,000,000. All of the goods had been sold by Wood plc by the end of the year.

- Dividends paid during the year were:
  - Wood plc, £1,500,000
  - Plank Limited, £800,000

- There were no impairment losses on goodwill during the year.

REQUIRED

Draft a consolidated income statement for Wood plc and its subsidiary undertaking for the year ended 31 March 20-1.

8.16   You have been asked to assist in the preparation of the consolidated accounts of the Jake Group. Set out on below are the balance sheets of Jake Limited and Dinos Limited as at 30 September 20–1:

Balance sheets as at 30 September 20-1

	Jake Ltd		Dinos Ltd	
	£000	£000	£000	£000
Tangible non-current assets		18,104		6,802
Investment in Dinos Limited		5,000		
Current assets	4,852		2,395	
Current liabilities	(2,376)		(547)	
Net current assets		2,476		1,848
Non-current (long-term) loan		(4,500)		(1,000)
Net assets		21,080		7,650
Equity				
Share capital		5,000		1,000
Share premium account		3,000		400
Retained earnings		13,080		6,250
Total equity		21,080		7,650

Further information:

- The share capital of both Jake Limited and Dinos Limited consists of ordinary shares of £1 each. There have been no changes to the balances of share capital and share premium during the year. No dividends were paid by Dinos Limited during the year.

- Jake Limited acquired 600,000 shares in Dinos Limited on 30 September 20-0.

- At 30 September 20-0 the retained earnings of Dinos Limited were £5,450,000.

- The fair value of the non-current assets of Dinos Limited at 30 September 20-0 was £3,652,000 as compared with their book value of £3,052,000. The revaluation has not been reflected in the books of Dinos Limited (ignore any depreciation implications).

- For the year to 30 September 20-1, Jake Limited has written off ten per cent of the goodwill on the acquisition of Dinos Limited as an impairment loss.

REQUIRED

You are to prepare the consolidated balance sheet of Jake Limited and its subsidiary undertaking as at 30 September 20-1.

Assignments

This section contains five assignments.

These assignments comprise sets of extended activities – sometimes based on more than one chapter – which consolidate learning and prepare the student for assessment.

Details of the assignments and chapter coverage are set out on the next page.

Note that blank photocopiable pro-formas are included in the Appendix; it is advisable to enlarge them up to full A4 size.

INTRODUCTION TO ASSIGNMENTS

These Assignments are designed to be used for practice as you progress through the *Limited Company Accounts (IAS) Tutorial* text. It is important to be able to apply the appropriate methods and techniques that you have learned to whatever scenario you may be given.

These Assignments therefore provide a variety of situations. The list below shows the relevant chapters which should be studied before attempting each Assignment.

This section is not intended to give complete coverage of Unit 11 on its own. Further practice can be gained by using the Workbook Activities and the Practice Examinations.

Assignment	relevant Tutorial chapters	page
1 DEALING WITH COMPANY ACCOUNTS Private and public limited company accounts	1, 2, 3	71
2 ADVISING ON ACCOUNTING POLICIES Accounting policies and accounting standards	4, 5	78

3   CASH FLOW STATEMENTS
    Preparing cash flow statements; interpretation
    of cash flow statements
	6	81

4 ACCOUNTING RATIOS Calculating and commenting on accounting ratios	7	84

5   CONSOLIDATED ACCOUNTS
    Preparing the consolidated income statement
    and balance sheet: dealing with associated
    companies, and fair value
	8	88

DEALING WITH COMPANY ACCOUNTS   1

SITUATION

You work for a firm of accountants, Swinburn Stanfield & Company. During the course of the week you have been given a number of tasks which relate to limited company accounts.

TASKS

1   Your first task of the week is to attend a board meeting of Vision Press Limited, a publisher of children's books. You have recently produced the draft financial statements of the company and the directors now wish to ask you a number of questions about the accounts. Prepare notes for the directors which will answer the following questions:

(a)   Why are inventories shown on the company balance sheet as a current asset, when it is a permanent asset of the business? The company is very careful in that it uses a buffer system which means that it will never run out of inventories completely. With this in mind wouldn't it make more sense to show inventories as a non-current asset on the balance sheet?

(b)   Why are the business premises shown as a non-current asset when in fact they are a liability to the business as we owe the bank a substantial amount of money on those premises in the form of a commercial mortgage? This must be the case, because the mortgage is listed under the heading non-current liabilities on the balance sheet?

(c)   The employees' representatives have requested a copy of the published accounts. Why would they want to see them?

2 The following trial balance has been extracted from the books of account for Sharjah plc as at 31 May 20-4:

	Dr	Cr
	£000	£000
Administrative expenses	250	
Distribution costs	170	
Wages and salaries	450	
Directors fees	170	
Rent, rates and insurance	160	
Bank interest	10	
Issued share capital		1,000
Trade receivables	700	
Cash and cash equivalents	30	
Bank overdraft		60
Share premium account		200
Interim dividend paid	120	
Buildings:		
At cost	2,000	
Accumulated depreciation at 1 June 20-3		400
Vehicles:		
At cost	1,000	
Accumulated depreciation at 1 June 20-3		500
Purchases	1,100	
Revenue		3,000
Trade payables		500
Inventories at 1 June 20-3	210	
Retained earnings at 1 June 20-3		710
	6,370	6,370

Additional information

- Inventories at 31 May 20-4 are valued at £230,000.
- The tax liabilities based on the profits for the year are £100,000.
- The company adopts the following policy with regard to depreciation:

    Buildings 2 per cent per annum on cost.

    Vehicles 25 per cent per annum on cost.

REQUIRED

(a)   Prepare the company's income statement (including a statement of the change in retained earnings) for the year to 31 May 20-4. (This is required for internal purposes only).

(b)   Explain briefly how the balance on the share premium account arose.

3   You have been assigned to assist in the preparation of the financial statements of McTaggart Limited for the year ended 30 April 20-4. The company markets and distributes its board game called 'The Absolute' to a worldwide market from its premises in Cambridge.

You have been provided with an extract from the extended trial balance of McTaggart Limited on 30 April 20-4 (set out on the next page).

You have been given the following further information:

•   the authorised share capital of the business, all of which has been issued, consists of ordinary shares with a nominal value of £1

•   depreciation has been calculated on all of the non-current assets of the business and has already been entered on a monthly basis into the distribution costs and administrative expenses ledger balances as shown on the extended trial balance

•   the corporation tax charge for the year has been calculated as £1,113,000

•   interest on the long-term loan has not been paid for the last month of the year; the interest charge for April 20-4 amounts to £26,000

REQUIRED

Taking into account the further information provided, draft an income statement (including a statement of the change in retained earnings) for the year ended 30 April 20-4 and a balance sheet as at that date.

Notes

•   you are not required to produce journal entries for any adjustments to the figures in the extended trial balance, but you may find them useful as working notes

•   ignore any effect of these adjustments on the tax charge for the year as given above

EXTENDED TRIAL BALANCE (extract) name: McTaggart Ltd date: 30 April 20-4				
Description	**Income statement**		**Balance sheet**	
	Dr *£000*	*Cr* *£000*	*Dr* *£000*	*Cr* *£000*
Trade payables				1,891
Retained earnings				2,159
Dividends paid*	240			
Land – cost			1,820	
Buildings – cost			2,144	
Fixtures and fittings – cost			1,704	
Vehicles – cost			1,931	
Office equipment – cost			236	
Trade receivables			2,191	
Interest	166			
Revenue		15,373		
Accruals				145
Provision for doubtful receivables				85
Distribution costs	2,033			
Administrative expenses	1,562			
Inventories	2,034	4,731	4,731	
Cash and cash equivalents			1,086	
Long-term loan				2,750
Returns inwards	95			
Returns outwards		157		
Buildings – accumulated depreciation				872
Fixtures and fittings – accumulated dep'n				898
Vehicles – accumulated dep'n				1,027
Office equipment – accumulated dep'n				88
Share capital				3,000
Purchases	11,166			
Prepayments			37	
Profit	2,965			2,965
	20,261	20,261	15,880	15,880

* deducted from profit

4   You have been assigned to assist in the preparation of the financial statements of Primavera Fashions Limited for the year ended 31 March 20-4. The company is a trading company which distributes fashion clothing.

Primavera Fashions Limited recently engaged a financial accountant to manage a team of book-keepers. The book-keepers produced a correct extended trial balance of the company and gave it to the accountant so that he could draft the year end financial statements.

The book-keeping staff have reported that he appeared to have some difficulty with the task and, after several days, apparently gave up the task and has not been seen since. He left behind him a balance sheet and some pages of workings which appear to contain a number of errors.

There is to be a meeting of the Board next week at which the financial statements will be approved. You have been brought in to assist in the production of a corrected balance sheet. The uncorrected balance sheet, the workings left by the financial accountant and an extract from the extended trial balance (which *is* correct) of Primavera Fashions Limited on 31 March 20-4 are set out on the next three pages.

EXTENDED TRIAL BALANCE (extract)	name: Primavera Fashions Limited date: 31 March 20-4			
Description	**Income statement**		**Balance sheet**	
	Dr *£000*	*Cr* *£000*	*Dr* *£000*	*Cr* *£000*
Retained earnings				2,852
Land – revaluation			1,525	
Buildings – cost			1,000	
Fixtures and fittings – cost			1,170	
Vehicles – cost			1,520	
Office equipment – cost			350	
Revenue		12,604		
Buildings – accumulated depreciation				220
Fixtures and fittings – accumulated dep'n				346
Vehicles – accumulated dep'n				583
Office equipment – accumulated dep'n				143
Inventories	1,097	1,178	1,178	
Interest	153			
Goodwill			128	
Trade receivables			857	
Purchases	7,604			
Dividends paid*	160			
Investments			2,924	
Cash and cash equivalents			152	
Distribution costs	1,495			
Administrative expenses	1,457			
Depreciation – buildings	50			
Depreciation – fixtures and fittings	117			
Depreciation – vehicles	380			
Depreciation – office equipment	70			
Share capital				2,000
Provision for doubtful receivables				61
Trade payables				483
Accruals				104
Prepayments			37	
10% Debentures				1,500
Share premium account				800
Revaluation reserve				550
Profit	1,199			1,199
	13,782	13,782	10,841	10,841

* deducted from profit

PRIMAVERA FASHIONS LIMITED

Balance Sheet as at 31 March 20-4

	£000	£000
Non-current assets		
Goodwill		128
Tangible assets[1]		4,948
Investments		2,924
		8,000
Current assets		
Inventories	1,097	
Trade and other receivables[2]	924	
Cash and cash equivalents	152	
	2,173	
Current liabilities		
Trade and other payables[3]	(2,044)	
Tax liabilities	(382)	
	(2,426)	
Net current liabilities		(253)
		7,747
Non-current liabilities		
Share premium account		(800)
Net assets		6,947
Equity		
Share capital		2,000
Revaluation reserve[4]		550
Retained earnings[5]		4,051
Total equity		6,601

workings

1   **Non-current tangible assets**

	Cost/ Revaluation	Accumulated depreciation	Net book value
	£000	£000	£000
Land	1,525	–	1,525
Buildings	1,000	50	950
Fixtures and fittings	1,170	117	1,053
Vehicles	1,520	380	1,140
Office equipment	350	70	280
	5,565	617	4,948

2   Trade and other receivables

	£000
Trade receivables	857
Accruals	104
	961
Prepayments	(37)
	924

3   Trade and other payables

	£000
Trade payables	483
Provision for doubtful receivables	61
10% Debentures	1,500
	2,044

4   The revaluation reserve comes from the revaluation of the land during the year from a cost of £975,000 to a valuation of £1,525,000.

5   Retained earnings

	£000
At 1 April 20-3	2,852
Profit for the year	1,199
At 31 March 20-4	4,051

You have also received the following additional information to assist you in your task:

*   The tax liabilities for the year are £382,000.

*   The investments shown on the extended trial balance relate to a long-term investment in the shares of a subsidiary company.

REQUIRED

(a)   Redraft the company balance sheet for Primavera Fashions Limited as at 31 March 20-4. Make any changes that you feel to be necessary to the balance sheet and workings provided by the disappearing financial accountant using the information contained in the extended trial balance for the year ended 31 March 20-4 and the additional information provided above. The balance sheet should meet the requirements of the applicable international accounting standards.

(b)   Prepare a statement of recognised income and expense for Primavera Fashions Limited for the year ended 31 March 20-4 as required by IAS 1.

ADVISING ON ACCOUNTING POLICIES 2

SITUATION

You work for the accounting firm Wasserman Pricehaus. You have a number of clients who find it difficult understanding accounting concepts and the idea of accounting for assets and liabilities and profit. Last week you had three clients with queries about their financial statements.

TASKS

1   Joseph Coxhead is the owner of his own fine art gallery business, Coxhead & Company Limited. He has recently received his latest set of financial statements and has prepared a list of questions and queries for your attention.

The questions are as follows:

(a)   Why doesn't my balance sheet show my personal home as an asset? I conduct a lot of my business meetings and entertaining there, as well as producing a number of sketches in my spare time.

(b)   I have wanted to value all my art paintings this year at selling price, rather than cost price as this will give a higher profit figure and will impress my bank manager!

(c)   Last year I used the reducing balance method to calculate the depreciation on my delivery van, however this year I wanted to change to the straight-line method as this will reduce the charge for depreciation and increase my profit figure.

(d)   I was keen during the year to keep my dividends to a minimum, again to achieve as high as profit figure as possible. Hopefully this strategy has now paid off in the accounts.

(e)   I suspect that when I built the extension to the art gallery this year, some of the invoices were entered into the 'Art gallery at cost' account, but some of the others were entered into the 'Buildings repairs and maintenance' account. However I don't think that this matters too much as it will all be written off to the income statement eventually anyway.

REQUIRED

Comment on each of the points listed above made by Joseph and in each case where relevant refer to the relevant accounting concepts and international accounting standards.

2   You have received the following comments and suggestions from the Finance Director of Mason Holdings plc at a meeting held to discuss the information needed for the year's draft accounts:

(a)   "There is no point in depreciating the freehold buildings because the market value must be considerably in excess of its cost."

(b)   "I see that the gain in value of our investment property in Guildford has been credited to the income statement. I would prefer that we depreciate it at the same rate as our other properties, in line with the consistency concept in accountancy."

(c)   "The research undertaken by the company this year should be recognised on the balance sheet as deferred development expenditure. I know that the product is only at its early stages but I am hopeful that the project is a good idea and it could work for us in the future."

(d)   "During the year we acquired another company leading to some purchased goodwill. I suggest we write this off immediately to our reserves. There is no point in carrying forward in the accounts an asset that does not exist."

(e)   "This year we leased all of our vehicles under a finance lease for the first time. Reading through the contract, I see that the vehicles do not legally become ours until the final instalment has been paid, and then only when the option to purchase payment has been made. I therefore suggest that we treat all the payments made as a form of rent and charge them to the income statement accordingly."

REQUIRED

How would you reply to each of these points raised by the Finance Director? In each case offer advice as to the best accounting practice to be followed. You will need to refer to the relevant international accounting standards where applicable.

3   The directors of Maximilian PLC are about to approve the financial statements for the current year ending 31 August 20-4. Since the accounts were prepared, the following additional information has now been made available. Assume the date today is 19 October 20-4.

(a)   On 16 October an electrical fire caused severe damage to the company's factory which is likely to make the manufacturing process inoperable for the next three months.

(b)   The year end figure of trade receivables includes an amount of £15,000 from a customer who has been made bankrupt on 14 October. It is unlikely that any money will be received from this customer.

(c)   The company is currently awaiting the outcome of a legal case. An independent lawyer has assessed that it is probable that Maximilian PLC will receive £100,000 from it.

(d)   The company is expecting to receive an order from a customer in Tokyo in the next few days worth £10 million based on a new product which the company has just marketed and released.

(e)   A former employee is currently involved with legal action against the company over an alleged assault which took place after the Christmas party. The case is proving difficult to prove and the company's solicitors recommend that there is no likelihood of this action succeeding.

REQUIRED

Advise the directors, giving your reasons, as to how these situations should be dealt with in the company's financial statements for the year ended 31 August 20-4. Wherever possible you should refer to the relevant international accounting standards.

CASH FLOW STATEMENTS

3

SITUATION

You are an accounts assistant in the accounting firm Henman Osborne & Co. Your supervisor has handed you some tasks on cash flow statements. You are to carry out the tasks set and will then hand them to your supervisor so that she can see how you are getting on.

TASKS

1   You have been given the financial statements of Edlin Limited for the year ended 31 March 20-6, with comparative figures for the year ended 31 March 20-5. The company is expanding and is in the middle of a major programme of replacing all of its non-current assets.

Edlin Limited

Income statement for the year ended 31 March

	20-6		20-5	
	£000	£000	£000	£000
Revenue, continuing operations		3,000		2,000
Opening inventories	200		150	
Purchases	1,700		1,250	
Less Closing inventories	220		200	
Cost of sales		(1,680)		(1,200)
Gross profit		1,320		800
Depreciation		(175)		(150)
Other expenses		(500)		(400)
Gain on sale of non-current asset		5		–
Profit from operations		650		250
Interest paid		(15)		(12)
Profit before tax		635		238
Tax		(100)		(35)
Profit after tax		535		203

Edlin Limited

Balance sheet as at 31 March

	20-6		20-5	
	£000	£000	£000	£000
Non-current assets		552		200
Current assets				
Inventories	220		200	
Trade receivables	250		160	
Cash and cash equivalents	218		20	
	688		380	
Current liabilities				
Trade payables	(250)		(160)	
Tax liabilities	(100)		(35)	
	(350)		(195)	
Net current assets		338		185
		890		385
Non-current liabilities				
Long-term loan		(150)		(120)
Net assets		740		265
Equity				
Called up share capital		120		100
Share premium account		70		50
Retained earnings		550		115
Total equity		740		265

The following further information is provided:

• Dividends proposed were: £100,000 in 20-5, and £150,000 in 20-6. These dividends were paid in 20-6 and 20-7 respectively.

* In July 20-5 a non-current asset was sold which had originally cost £20,000 when it was purchased by the company in July 20-2. Non-current assets are depreciated on a straightline basis at 20%. The policy is to charge a full year's depreciation in the year of purchase and none in the year of sale.

• A new non-current asset was purchased for £535,000 during the year.

• Revenue sales and purchases were on credit with all other expenses (including interest) being paid in cash.

• There was a share issue during the year.

REQUIRED

(a) Prepare a reconciliation of profit from operations to net cash flow from operating activities for Edlin Limited for the year ended 31 March 20-6.

(b) Prepare a cash flow statement for Edlin Limited for the year ended 31 March 20-6 in accordance with IAS 7.

2 Your supervisor has asked you to comment on the decline in the cash balance of Roth Limited in the year to 30 April 20-6. The cash flow statement of Roth Limited is set out below to assist you in your analysis:

ROTH LIMITED CASH FLOW STATEMENT FOR THE YEAR ENDED 30 APRIL 20-6		
	£000	£000
Net cash (used in)/from operating activities (see below)		3,400
Cash flows from investing activities		
Purchase of non-current assets	(1,432)	
Proceeds from sale of non-current assets	373	
Net cash (used in)/from investing activities		(1,059)
Cash flows from financing activities		
Proceeds from long-term borrowings	1,050	
Dividends paid	(5,000)	
Net cash (used in)/from financing activities		(3,950)
Net increase/(decrease) in cash and cash equivalents		(1,609)
Cash and cash equivalents at beginning of year		1,843
Cash and cash equivalents at end of year		234

Reconciliation of profit from operations to net cash flow from operating activities for the year ended 30 April 20-6	
	£000
Profit from operations	8,763
Adjustments for:	
Depreciation for year	1,847
Increase in inventories	(36)
Increase in trade receivables	(3,584)
Decrease in trade payables	(1,031)
Cash (used in)/from operations	5,959
Interest paid	(542)
Income taxes paid	(2,017)
Net cash (used in)/from operating activities	3,400

Further information:

Revenue and purchases for the company were similar this year to last year.

REQUIRED

Using the cash flow statement and the further information prepare notes to explain why the cash balance has fallen in the year to April 20-6.

ACCOUNTING RATIOS

4

SITUATION

You work as an accounts assistant in the business advisory section of a firm of accountants, Hartley, Wintney & Co. Your supervisor, Nisha Gupta, has given you two tasks to be worked on.

TASKS

1   The directors of Mercia Printers Ltd, a medium-sized printing firm, have recently read the industry's trade magazine and seen an article quoting the following average ratios for the printing sector:

Return on capital employed (ROCE)	16%
Gearing ratio (debt/equity)	27%
Current ratio	1.8:1
Net profit percentage	8%
Payables payment period	62 days

The magazine article discusses the benefits of printing companies benchmarking their own performance against the sector's industrial average in order to assess overall performance and efficiency.

Your firm has just prepared the latest published accounts for the company, which are as follows:

Mercia Printers Limited
Income statement for the year ended 31 August 20-4

	£000
Revenue – Continuing operations	2,750
Cost of sales	(2,200)
GROSS PROFIT	550
Distribution costs	(140)
Administrative expenses	(210)
PROFIT FROM OPERATIONS	200
Finance costs	(63)
PROFIT BEFORE TAX	137
Tax	(41)
PROFIT FOR THE YEAR	96

Mercia Printers Limited
Balance Sheet as at 31 August 20-4

	£000	£000
NON-CURRENT ASSETS		450
CURRENT ASSETS		
Inventories	215	
Trade receivables	352	
Cash and cash equivalents	13	
	580	
CURRENT LIABILITIES		
Trade payables	(133)	
Tax liabilities	(41)	
	(174)	
NET CURRENT ASSETS		406
		856
NON-CURRENT LIABILITIES		(250)
NET ASSETS		606
EQUITY		
Share capital		240
Retained earnings		366
TOTAL EQUITY		606

NOTES TO THE ACCOUNTS

- Purchases for the year included in the cost of sales calculation amounted to £2,215,000.

- There were no preference shares in issue during the year.

REQUIRED

You have been asked by your supervisor to draft a report for the directors of Mercia Printers Limited, assessing the performance of the company.

The draft report should include:

(a) A calculation from the published accounts of Mercia Printers Limited of the appropriate ratios listed in the magazine article (see above). You should quote the formulas used and show detailed workings for each ratio.

(b) An assessment of the company's overall performance, comparing its ratios with the sector average.

2 Terry Paine, a client of Hartley, Wintney & Co, is deciding whether to lend some money to Russell Limited. He has asked for a comment on the financial position of the company. The financial statements of Russell Limited are set out below.

Russell Limited

Income statements for the year ended 31 July

	20-4	20-3
	£000	£000
Revenue	7,702	6,826
Cost of sales	(4,004)	(3,550)
Gross profit	3,698	3,276
Distribution costs	(1,564)	(1,474)
Administrative expenses	(1,030)	(982)
Profit from operations	1,104	820
Finance costs	(92)	(82)
Profit before tax	1,012	738
Tax	(252)	(184)
Profit for the year	760	554

Russell Limited

Balance sheets as at 31 July

	20-4		20-3	
	£000	£000	£000	£000
Non-current assets		8,744		8,682
Current assets				
Inventories	2,314		1,432	
Trade and other receivables	938		1,056	
Cash and cash equivalents	74		114	
	3,326		2,602	
Current liabilities				
Trade and other payables	(1,194)		(1,116)	
Tax liabilities	(252)		(184)	
	(1,446)		(1,300)	
Net current assets		1,880		1,302
Non-current (long-term) loan		(1,200)		(1,000)
Net assets		9,424		8,984
Equity				
Share capital		2,000		2,000
Retained earnings		7,424		6,984
Total equity		9,424		8,984

REQUIRED

Write a letter to Terry Paine that includes the following:

(a)   A calculation of the following ratios of Russell Limited for each of the two years:

- Current ratio

- Quick ratio/acid test

- Gearing ratio (debt/equity)

- Interest cover

(b)   An explanation of the meaning of each ratio.

(c)   A comment on the financial position of Russell Limited as shown by the ratios.

(d)   A comment on the way the financial position has changed over the two years covered by the financial statements.

(e)   A conclusion on whether Terry Paine should lend money to Russell Limited. Base your conclusion only on the ratios calculated and analysis performed.

CONSOLIDATED ACCOUNTS

5

SITUATION

You work for the accounting firm Clarke Paul & Co. You have been handed a number of assignments relating to groups of companies. The tasks involve preparing consolidated accounts and advising on policy.

TASKS

1   You have been sent the following summarised balance sheets for the Rain group of companies as at 30 September 20-4

	Rain PLC	Sleet PLC
	£000	£000
NON-CURRENT ASSETS		
Plant and equipment at net book value	236	30
Investment :		
40,000 ordinary shares of £1 each in Sleet PLC	184	
	420	30
CURRENT ASSETS		
Inventories	150	80
Trade receivables	250	20
Cash and cash equivalents	50	10
	450	110
CURRENT LIABILITIES		
Trade payables	(280)	(20)
NET ASSETS	590	120
EQUITY		
Ordinary shares of £1 each	500	50
Retained earnings	90	70
TOTAL EQUITY	590	120

Additional information

- Rain acquired its shares in Sleet on 1 October 20-1 when Sleet's retained earnings amounted to £30,000.

- The respective company's trade receivables and trade payables at 30 September 20-4 include the following inter-company debt:

  Sleet owed Rain £5,000

- Ten per cent of any goodwill arising upon consolidation is to be written off each year on a straight-line basis as an impairment loss.

REQUIRED

Prepare Rain's consolidated balance sheet as at 30 September 20-4.

2   You are presented with the following summarised income statements for Norberry PLC and its subsidiary, Manberry Limited.

Income statements for the year ending 30 September 20-4

	Norberry PLC	Manberry Limited
	£000	£000
Revenue, continuing operations	1,700	450
Cost of sales	(920)	(75)
GROSS PROFIT	780	375
Distribution costs	(100)	(75)
Administrative expenses	(200)	(100)
PROFIT FROM OPERATIONS	480	200
Dividends received from Manberry Limited	120	–
PROFIT BEFORE TAX	600	200
Tax	(30)	(20)
PROFIT FOR THE YEAR	570	180

Additional information

- Norberry PLC acquired 80% of the shares in Manberry Limited on 1 October 20-1.

- During the year Norberry PLC sold goods which had cost £100,000 to Manberry Limited for £110,000. All the goods had been sold by Manberry Limited by the end of the year.

- Dividends paid during the year were:
  Norberry PLC, £360,000
  Manberry Limited, £150,000

- There were no impairment losses on goodwill during the year.

REQUIRED

(a) Draft a consolidated income statement for Norberry PLC and its subsidiary undertaking for the year ended 30 September 20-4.

(b) One of the directors subsequently telephoned asking about the entries for goodwill and minority interest. Briefly explain what both of these terms mean in relation to a consolidated balance sheet.

3 You are handed a query about the accounting treatment of associated companies. Charlton Limited purchased 30 per cent of the ordinary share capital of Kingley Limited for £280,000 on 1 October 20-3. Kingley Limited is an associated undertaking and the directors would like to know how Kingley Limited would be included in the consolidated income statement and consolidated balance sheet of the Charlton Group. Extracts from Kingley Limited's financial statements are given below:

Income statement of Kingley Limited for the year ended 30 September 20-4

	£000
Profit before tax	350
Tax	95
Profit for the year	255

Balance sheet of Kingley Limited as at 30 September 20-4

	£000
Non-current assets	800
Net current assets	150
	950
Non-current liability	(70)
	880
Equity	
Ordinary share capital	300
Share premium account	70
Retained earnings	510
Total equity	880

Notes

- no shares were issued in the year ended 30 September 20-4

- no dividends were paid or proposed in that year

- all assets of Kingley Limited are stated at fair values

- there were no impairment losses on goodwill during the year

REQUIRED

What figures would be shown in the consolidated income statement and consolidated balance sheet of the Charlton Group for the year ended 30 September 20-4 to account for the results of the associate Kingley Limited?

4 The Managing Director of Predator Limited, one of your clients, telephones to say that his company is about to acquire a majority shareholding in Minimus Limited. He has heard that the idea of 'fair value' is very important when it comes to asset valuation in a takeover situation.

Explain the concept of fair value in relation to an acquisition of another company.

Practice Examinations

This section contains assessment tasks derived from past Examinations for Unit 11, reproduced by kind permission of AAT.

Details of these practice examinations are set out on the next page.

PRACTICE EXAMINATIONS

A NOTE ON PRACTICE EXAMINATION TASKS

Osborne Books is grateful to the AAT for its kind permission to reproduce assessment tasks from past examinations for Unit 11. These practice examination tasks have been amended to incorporate the requirements of international accounting standards. In a number of cases dates and numbers have been changed to provide consistency of presentation.

As far as possible the guidance timings have been preserved. The 'pro-forma' documents found in the AAT answer booklets have been included in the Appendix (page 129). Before commencing a practice examination, students are advised to photocopy the required documents (enlarging them to A4 size). The guidance timings and the 'pro-forma' documents will enable students to gain familiarity with the way in which an examination 'works'.

An important note of caution: AAT is rightly anxious to point out that students should not 'question spot' likely topics for assessment and ignore other topics. They do so at their peril. Students should cover all areas of the specifications and so be technically competent in their studies – and in their work.

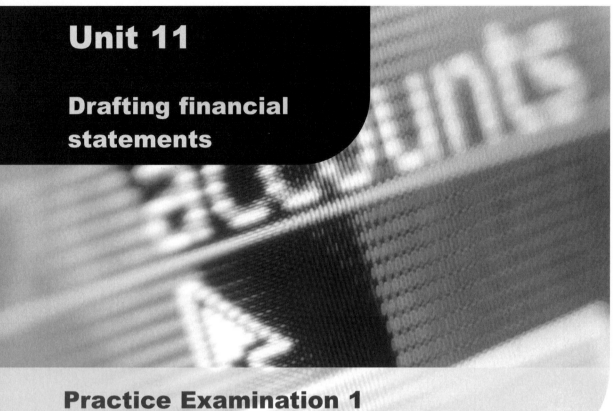

Unit 11

Drafting financial statements

Practice Examination 1
Murdoch Group; Okri Ltd; Bragg Plc

Element coverage

11.1   draft limited company financial statements

11.2   interpret limited company financial statements

Suggested time allocation

Three hours plus fifteen minutes reading time.

PRACTICE EXAMINATION 1
MURDOCH GROUP; OKRI LTD; BRAGG PLC

This Examination is in two sections.

You have to show competence in both sections.

You should therefore attempt and aim to complete every task in both sections.

You should spend about 125 minutes on section 1 and 55 minutes on section 2.

The following pro-forma is given in the Appendix:

• a consolidated balance sheet

SECTION 1

You should spend about 125 minutes on this section.
This section is in three parts.

PART A
You should spend about 50 minutes on this part.

DATA

You have been asked to help prepare the consolidated accounts of the Murdoch Group, and to advise the directors on accounting issues. The balance sheets of Murdoch plc and Lively Limited for the year ended 31 March 20-4 are set out on the next page.

Balance sheets as at 31 March 20-4

	Murdoch plc		Lively Ltd	
	£000	£000	£000	£000
Tangible non-current assets		24,831		9,831
Investment in Lively Ltd		9,000		
Current assets	11,487		4,652	
Current liabilities	(6,013)		(1,995)	
Net current assets		5,474		2,657
Non-current (long-term) loan		(7,500)		(2,500)
		31,805		9,988
Equity				
Share capital		9,000		2,000
Share premium account		4,000		1,000
Retained earnings		18,805		6,988
Total equity		31,805		9,988

You also have the following information:

- The share capital of both Murdoch plc and Lively Limited consists of ordinary shares of £1 each. There have been no changes to the balances of share capital and share premium account during the year. No dividends were paid or proposed by Lively Limited during the year.

- Murdoch plc acquired 1,500,000 shares in Lively Limited on 1 April 20-3.

- At 1 April 20-3 the balance of retained earnings of Lively Limited was £4,480,000.

- The fair value of the non-current assets of Lively Limited at 1 April 20-3 was £8,320,000 as compared with their book value of £5,320,000. The revaluation has not been reflected in the books of Lively Limited. (Ignore any depreciation implications.)

- Ten per cent of the goodwill arising on consolidation is to be written off as an impairment loss in the year to 31 March 20-4.

Task 1.1

Prepare the consolidated balance sheet of Murdoch plc and its subsidiary undertaking as at 31 March 20–4.

Task 1.2

The directors of Murdoch plc are considering whether to revalue some of Murdoch plc's non-current assets. Prepare brief notes for the directors to answer the following questions:

(a) If we adopt a policy of revaluation of land and buildings, do we have to revalue all our tangible non-current assets?

(b) If we adopt a policy of revaluation of some of Murdoch plc's land and buildings, do we have to revalue all the land and buildings?

(c) If we adopt a policy of revaluation for tangible non-current assets, what would be the carrying amount of the assets in the balance sheet?

(d) How often would we have to value properties if we adopt a policy of revaluation?

PART B

You are advised to spend about 40 minutes on this part.

DATA

The directors of Okri Limited have asked you to explain some aspects of the cash flow statement for the year ended 31 March 20-4. The directors have noted that, although the income statement shows that profit for the year was £2,812,000, the cash balance has actually decreased during the year by £807,000. They do not understand how this could have happened. The cash flow statement and the income statements and balance sheets of the company are set out below.

Okri Limited
Income statement for the year ended 31 March

	20-4		20-3	
	£000	£000	£000	£000
Revenue		10,213		10,359
Opening inventories	1,550		1,490	
Purchases	5,366		5,302	
Less Closing inventories	2,320		1,550	
Cost of sales		(4,596)		(5,242)
Gross profit		5,617		5,117
Distribution costs		(936)		(942)
Administrative expenses		(581)		(597)
Profit from operations		4,100		3,578
Interest paid		(400)		(80)
Profit before tax		3,700		3,498
Tax		(888)		(840)
Profit for the year		2,812		2,658

Okri Limited
Balance sheet as at 31 March

	20-4		20-3	
	£000	£000	£000	£000
Non-current assets		12,199		6,729
Current assets				
Inventories	2,320		1,550	
Trade receivables	2,553		1,944	
Cash and cash equivalents	87		894	
	4,960		4,388	
Current liabilities				
Trade payables	(1,045)		(1,263)	
Tax liabilities	(888)		(840)	
	(1,933)		(2,103)	
Net current assets		3,027		2,285
Non-current liabilities				
Long-term loan		(5,000)		(1,000)
		10,226		8,014
Equity				
Called up share capital		2,000		2,000
Retained earnings		8,226		6,014
Total equity		10,226		8,014

Further information:

- The total depreciation charge for the year to 31 March 20-4 was £930,000.

- All revenue sales and purchases were on credit. Other expenses were paid for in cash.

- Dividends proposed were £600,000 in 20-3 and £1,200,000 in 20-4. These dividends were paid in 20–4 and 20-5 respectively.

Okri Limited
Cash flow statement for the year ended 31 March 20-4

	£000	£000
Net cash (used in)/from operating activities		2,193
Cash flows from investing activities		
Purchase of non-current assets	(6,400)	
Net cash (used in)/from investing activities		(6,400)
Cash flows from financing activities		
Proceeds from long-term borrowings	4,000	
Dividends paid	(600)	
Net cash (used in)/from financing activities		3,400
Net increase/(decrease) in cash and cash equivalents		(807)
Cash and cash equivalents at beginning of year		894
Cash and cash equivalents at end of year		87

Task 1.3

Prepare a reconciliation of profit from operations to net cash flows from operating activities for Okri Limited for the year ended 31 March 20-4.

Task 1.4

Draft a letter to the directors of Okri Limited explaining why the cash balance has fallen in the year ended 31 March 20-4, even though there was a substantial profit for the year. For your answer, use only the information in the financial statements of the business, including the cash flow statement, and the reconciliation of profit from operations to net cash flows from operating activities.

PART C

You are advised to spend about 35 minutes on this part.

DATA

IAS 1, *Presentation of Financial Statements*, requires the disclosure of accounting policies in the notes to the accounts.

Task 1.5

Explain why the disclosure of accounting policies is useful to users of accounts. Illustrate your answer with reference to:

(a)   depreciation

(b)   research and development

(c)   inventories

SECTION 2

You are advised to spend about 55 minutes on this section.

DATA

Bragg plc wants to acquire a majority holding in a private limited company. The Managing Director of Bragg plc has asked you to analyse the financial statements of two possible companies and to deal with some queries he has about financial statements. He has asked you to consider the profitability of the companies and their financial position. The financial statements of the two companies are set out below and on the next page.

Summary Income statements
for the year ended 31 March 20-4

	Roy Limited	Ishiguro Limited
	£000	£000
Revenue	8,483	10,471
Cost of sales	(3,732)	(5,026)
Gross profit	4,751	5,445
Distribution costs	(1,218)	(1,483)
Administrative expenses	(903)	(1,658)
Profit from operations	2,630	2,304
Finance costs	(160)	(520)
Profit before tax	2,470	1,784
Tax	(593)	(428)
Profit for the year	1,877	1,356
Dividends paid in year	400	800

Balance sheets as at 31 March 20-4

	Roy Limited		Ishiguro Limited	
	£000	£000	£000	£000
Non-current assets		6,806		12,579
Current assets				
Inventories	2,531		2,181	
Trade receivables	1,054		2,309	
Cash and cash equivalents	828		5	
	4,413		4,495	
Current liabilities				
Trade payables	(1,259)		(2,166)	
Bank overdraft	–		(483)	
Tax liabilities	(593)		(428)	
	(1,852)		(3,077)	
Net current assets		2,561		1,418
Non-current liabilities				
Long-term loan		(2,000)		(6,500)
		7,367		7,497
Equity				
Called up share capital		2,000		2,000
Share premium account		1,000		500
Retained earnings		4,367		4,997
Total equity		7,367		7,497

Task 2.1

Prepare a report for Bragg plc that includes the following:

(a)   a calculation of the following four ratios of Roy Limited and Ishiguro Limited:

return on equity, gross profit percentage, gearing (debt/equity), interest cover

(b)   an explanation of the meaning of each ratio and a comment on the relative profitability and financial position of the two companies based on the ratios calculated

(c)   a conclusion as to which company to invest in, based only on these ratios and your analysis

Task 2.2

In an appendix to your report, answer the Managing Director's queries.

(a)   Use the accounting equation to demonstrate the monetary value of the equity in Roy Limited as at 31 March 2-4.

(b)   What is the objective of financial statements according to the *Framework for the Preparation and Presentation of Financial Statements*?

(c)   Give TWO examples of types of external users of financial statements. For each user, identify their purpose in using information in financial statements.

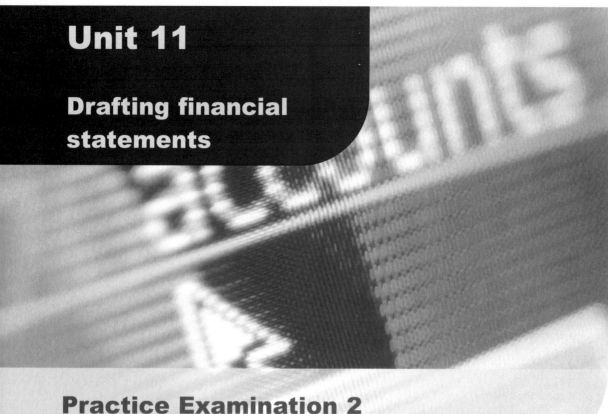

Unit 11

Drafting financial statements

Practice Examination 2
Skuhn plc; Paton Ltd; Quine Ltd; Goodall Ltd

Element coverage

11.1   draft limited company financial statements

11.2   interpret limited company financial statements

Suggested time allocation

Three hours plus fifteen minutes' reading time.

PRACTICE EXAMINATION 2
SKUHN PLC; PATON LTD; QUINE LTD; GOODALL LTD

This Examination is in two sections.

You have to show competence in both sections.

You should therefore attempt and aim to complete every task in both sections.

You should spend about 125 minutes on section 1, and 55 minutes on section 2.

The following pro-formas are given in the Appendix:

- a consolidated income statement

- a company cash flow statement

- a company balance sheet

- a statement of recognised income and expense

SECTION 1

You should spend about 125 minutes on this section.

This section is in four parts.

PART A

You should spend about 30 minutes on this part.

DATA

The Managing Director of Skuhn plc has asked you to prepare the draft consolidated income statement for the group. The company has one subsidiary undertaking, e-Lakatos Limited. The income statements for the two companies prepared for internal purposes for the year ended 30 September 20-4 are set out on the next page.

Income statements for the year ended 30 September 20-4

	Skuhn plc	e-Lakatos Limited
	£000	£000
Revenue	25,300	8,600
Cost of sales	(11,385)	(3,870)
Gross profit	13,915	4,730
Distribution costs	(3,655)	(985)
Administrative expenses	(2,730)	(320)
Dividends received from e-Lakatos Limited	600	–
Profit from operations	8,130	3,425
Finance costs	(2,100)	(400)
Profit before tax	6,030	3,025
Tax	(1,870)	(695)
Profit for the year	4,160	2,330

Further information:

- Skuhn plc acquired 60% of the ordinary share capital of e-Lakatos Limited on 1 October 20-3.

- During the year e-Lakatos Limited sold goods which had cost £800,000 to Skuhn plc for £1,200,000. All of the goods had been sold by Skuhn plc by the end of the year.

- Dividends paid during the year were:

    Skuhn plc, £2,100,000

    e-Lakatos Limited, £1,000,000

- There were no impairment losses on goodwill during the year.

Task 1.1

Draft a consolidated income statement for Skuhn plc and its subsidiary undertaking for the year ended 30 September 20-4.

PART B

You are advised to spend 35 minutes on this part.

DATA

You have been asked to assist in the preparation of financial statements for Paton Limited for the year ended 30 September 20-4. The income statement and balance sheets of Paton Limited are set out below.

Paton Limited
Income statement for the year ended 30 September 20-4

	£000
Revenue	24,732
Cost of sales	(11,129)
Gross profit	13,603
Gain on the sale of non-current assets	131
Distribution costs	(4,921)
Administrative expenses	(2,875)
Profit from operations	5,938
Finance costs	(392)
Profit before tax	5,546
Tax	(1,821)
Profit for the year	3,725

Paton Limited

Balance sheet as at 30 September

	20-4		20-3	
	£000	£000	£000	£000
Non-current assets		13,383		9,923
Investment in MacNeal Limited (non-current)		5,000		–
Current assets				
Inventories	7,420		6,823	
Trade receivables	4,122		3,902	
Cash and cash equivalents	102		1,037	
	11,644		11,762	
Current liabilities				
Trade payables	(2,755)		(2,132)	
Tax liabilities	(1,821)		(1,327)	
	(4,576)		(3,459)	
Net current assets		7,068		8,303
Non-current liabilities				
Long-term loan		(5,000)		(1,500)
Net assets		20,451		16,726
Equity				
Called up share capital		10,000		9,000
Share premium account		3,500		3,000
Retained earnings		6,951		4,726
Total equity		20,451		16,726

You have been given the following further information:

- A non-current asset costing £895,000 with accumulated depreciation of £372,000 was sold in the year. The total depreciation charge for the year was £2,007,000.

- Dividends proposed were: £1,500,000 in 20-3 and £2,000,000 in 20-4. These dividends were paid in 20-4 and 20-5 respectively.

- All revenue sales and purchases were on credit. Other expenses were paid for in cash.

Task 1.2

Prepare a reconciliation of profit from operations to net cash flow from operating activities for Paton Limited for the year ended 30 September 20-4.

Task 1.3

Prepare a cash flow statement for Paton Limited for the year ended 30 September 20-4 in accordance with IAS 7.

PART C

You are advised to spend 15 minutes on this part.

DATA

Paton Limited, the company in Tasks 1.2 and 1.3, has one subsidiary undertaking, MacNeal Limited, which it acquired on 30 September 20-4. The balance sheet of MacNeal Limited as at 30 September is set out below.

MacNeal Limited
Balance sheet as at 30 September 20-4

	£000	£000
Non-current assets		4,844
Current assets	3,562	
Current liabilities	(1,706)	
Net current assets		1,856
Non-current (long-term) loan		(1,900)
Net assets		4,800
Equity		
Called up share capital		1,200
Share premium account		800
Retained earnings		2,800
Total equity		4,800

You have been given the following further information:

- The share capital of MacNeal Limited consists of ordinary shares of £1 each.

- Paton Limited acquired 900,000 shares in MacNeal Limited on 30 September 20-4 at a cost of £5,000,000.

- The fair value of the non-current assets of MacNeal Limited at 30 September 20-4 was £5,844,000. The revaluation has not been reflected in the books of MacNeal Limited.

Task 1.4

Calculate the goodwill on consolidation that arose on the acquisition of MacNeal Limited on 30 September 20-4.

PART D

You are advised to spend 45 minutes on this part.

DATA

The Chief Accountant of Quine Limited has asked you to help prepare the financial statements for the year ended 30 September 20-4. The trial balance of the company as at 30 September 20-4 is set out below.

Quine Limited
Trial balance as at 30 September 20-4

	Debit	Credit
	£000	£000
Ordinary share capital		3,000
Interest	200	
Trade receivables	1,802	
Dividends paid	600	
Non-current (long-term) loan		2,500
Distribution costs	980	
Administrative expenses	461	
Revenue		10,884
Retained earnings at 1 October 20-3		1,457
Cash and cash equivalents	103	
Accruals		105
Prepayments	84	
Share premium account		500
Land – cost	2,800	
Buildings – cost	1,480	
Fixtures and fittings – cost	645	
Vehicles – cost	1,632	
Office equipment – cost	447	
Buildings – accumulated depreciation		702
Fixtures and fittings – accumulated depreciation		317
Vehicles – accumulated depreciation		903
Office equipment – accumulated depreciation		182
Inventories at 1 October 20-3	2,003	
Trade payables		1,309
Purchases	7,854	
Provision for doubtful receivables		72
Capitalised development expenditure	840	
	21,931	21,931

Further information:

- The inventories at the close of business on 30 September 20-4 were valued at cost at £2,382,000.

- The tax liabilities for the year are £548,000.

- The land has been revalued by professional valuers at £3,200,000. The revaluation is to be included in the financial statements for the year ended 30 September 20-4.

Task 1.5

(a)   Making any adjustments required as a result of the further information provided, draft a balance sheet for Quine Limited at 30 September 20-4.

   Note: 1.   You are not required to produce notes to the accounts.

   2.   You must show any workings relevant to understanding your calculation of figures appearing in the financial statements.

   3.   You are not required to produce journal entries for any adjustments required to the figures in the trial balance.

(b)   Prepare a statement of recognised income and expense for Quine Limited for the year ended 30 September 20-4 as required by IAS 1.

DATA

The Chief Accountant of Quine Limited tells you that the company is shortly to sign a lease with a finance company for some new vehicles. She knows that the accounting treatment of these will differ from other non-current assets. However, she is not sure how the year end financial statements will be affected and has asked you to clarify certain aspects of accounting for leases. She has arranged a meeting with you to discuss these matters.

Task 1.6

Prepare notes for the meeting covering the following matters:

(a)   Briefly differentiate between the two main types of lease.

(b)   Explain the accounting procedures for the two main types of lease, referring to any applicable international accounting standards.

SECTION 2

You are advised to spend about 55 minutes on this section.

This section is in two parts.

PART A

You should spend about 40 minutes on this part.

DATA

Michael Beacham has been asked to lend money to Goodall Limited for a period of three years. He employed a financial adviser to advise him whether to make a loan to the company. The financial adviser has obtained the financial statements of the company for the past two years, calculated some ratios and found the industry averages. However, she was unable to complete her report. Michael has asked you to analyse the ratios and to advise him on whether he should make a loan to Goodall Limited. The ratios are set out below.

	20-4	20-3	Industry average
Gearing ratio (debt/equity)	67%	58%	41%
Interest cover	1.2	2.3	4.6
Quick ratio/acid test	0.5	0.8	1.1
Return on equity	9%	13%	19%

Task 2.1

Write a report for Michael Beacham that includes the following:

(a)   an explanation of the meaning of each ratio

(b)   a comment on Goodall Limited's financial position and the financial performance of the company as shown by the ratios

(c)   a statement of how the financial position and performance have changed over the two years, and how they compare with the industry average

(d)   a conclusion on whether Michael should lend money to Goodall Limited; base your conclusion only on the ratios calculated and the analysis performed

PART B

You should spend about 15 minutes on this part.

DATA

The *Framework for the Preparation and Presentation of financial Statements* says that:

'The objective of financial statements is to provide information about the financial position, performance and changes in financial position of an entity that is useful to a wide range of users in making economic decisions.'

The *Framework* also identifies the elements of financial statements as being:

- assets
- liabilities
- equity
- income
- expenses

Task 2.2

(a)   Explain how the objective of financial statements has been met in the situation set out in Part A above.

(b)   (i)   In which financial statement are "assets", "liabilities" and "equity" shown?

(ii)   How are they related to each other in that statement?

(c)   What is meant by "income" and "expenses" and in which financial statement are they normally shown?

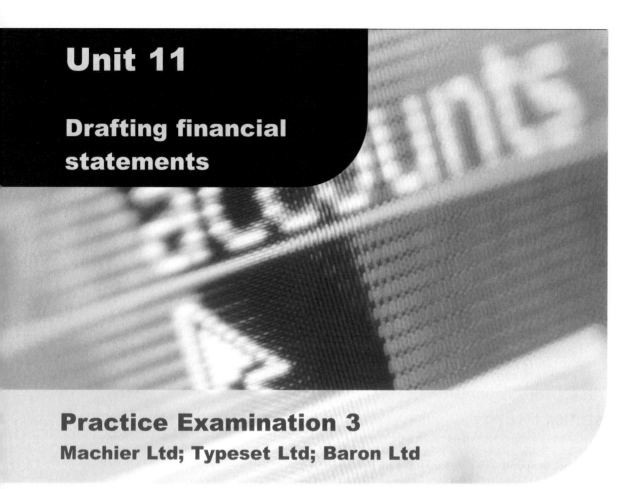

Unit 11

Drafting financial statements

Practice Examination 3
Machier Ltd; Typeset Ltd; Baron Ltd

Element coverage

11.1   draft limited company financial statements

11.2   interpret limited company financial statements

Suggested time allocation

Three hours plus fifteen minutes' reading time.

PRACTICE EXAMINATION 3
MACHIER LTD; TYPESET LTD; BARON LTD

This Examination is in two sections.

You have to show competence in both sections.

You should therefore attempt and aim to complete every task in both sections.

You should spend about 125 minutes on section 1, and 55 minutes on section 2.

The following pro-formas are given in the Appendix:

- a consolidated balance sheet
- a journal
- a statement of recognised income and expense
- a company cash flow statement

SECTION 1

You should spend about 125 minutes on this section.

This section is in three parts.

PART A

You should spend about 55 minutes on this part.

DATA

The directors of Machier Limited have asked you to assist them in producing a cash flow statement for the year ended 31 March 20-4 using the information in the balance sheet and income statement shown on the next two pages.

The following further information is also provided:

- non-current assets costing £28,000 with accumulated depreciation of £19,000 were sold in the year
- dividends proposed were: £40,000 in 20-3 and £50,000 in 20-4. These dividends were paid in 20-4 and 20-5 respectively.
- all revenue sales and purchases were on credit; other expenses were paid for in cash

The directors have also been in negotiation with the directors of another company, Papier Limited, about the possibility of Papier Limited buying 75 per cent of the share capital of Machier Limited. If the acquisition goes ahead, Papier Limited will pay £1,761,000 for the shares based on the value of the company as at 31 March 20-4. The fair value of the non-current assets in Machier Limited at 31 March 20-4, the agreed date of acquisition, is £4,682,000. All of the other assets and liabilities are stated at fair value. There is a meeting of the directors of both companies shortly. The directors of Machier Limited wish you to attend this meeting to explain some of the accounting issues involved in the acquisition of Machier Limited by Papier Limited.

Task 1.1

Provide a reconciliation of profit from operations to net cash flows from operating activities for Machier Limited for the year ended 31 March 20-4.

Task 1.2

Prepare a cash flow statement for Machier Limited for the year ended 31 March 20-4 in accordance with IAS 7.

Task 1.3

Calculate the goodwill on consolidation that would arise on acquisition if Papier Limited had purchased 75 per cent of the shares in Machier Limited on 31 March 20-4.

Note: you are not required to produce a consolidated balance sheet for the group.

Task 1.4

In a note to the directors, explain the accounting treatment of goodwill arising on acquisition in group accounts.

Machier Limited
Income statement for the year ended 31 March

	20-4	20-3
	£000	£000
Revenue	2,636	1,687
Cost of sales	(923)	(590)
Gross profit	1,713	1,097
Depreciation	(856)	(475)
Other expenses	(126)	(101)
Gain on the sale of non-current assets	7	2
Profit from operations	738	523
Finance costs	(252)	(120)
Profit before tax	486	403
Tax	(165)	(137)
Profit for the year	321	266

Machier Limited
Balance sheet as at 31 March

	20-4	20-3
	£000	£000
Non-current assets	4,282	2,376
Current assets		
Inventories	448	287
Trade receivables	527	337
Cash and cash equivalents	–	86
	975	710
Current liabilities		
Trade payables	(401)	(222)
Tax liabilities	(165)	(137)
Bank overdraft	(183)	–
	(749)	(359)
Net current assets	226	351
Non-current assets		
Long-term loan	(2,800)	(1,500)
	1,708	1,227
Equity		
Called up share capital	200	100
Share premium account	100	–
Retained earnings	1,408	1,127
Total equity	1,708	1,227

PART B

You are advised to spend about 50 minutes on this part.

DATA

You have been assigned to assist in the preparation of the financial statements of Typeset Limited for the year ended 31 March 20-4. The company is a wholesale distributor of desktop publishing equipment. You have been provided with the trial balance of Typeset Limited as at 31 March 20-4.

	Dr	Cr
	£000	£000
Trade receivables	3,136	
Cash and cash equivalents	216	
Interest	58	
Retained earnings at 1 April 20-3		3,533
Provision for doubtful receivables		37
Distribution costs	3,549	
Administrative expenses	3,061	
Revenue		19,257
Land – cost	2,075	
Buildings – cost	2,077	
Fixtures and fittings – cost	1,058	
Vehicles – cost	2,344	
Office equipment – cost	533	
Inventories at 1 April 20-3	3,921	
Purchases	10,649	
Dividends paid	250	
Trade payables		1,763
Buildings – accumulated depreciation		383
Fixtures and fittings – accumulated depreciation		495
Vehicles – accumulated depreciation		1,237
Office equipment – accumulated depreciation		152
Ordinary share capital		5,000
Share premium account		1,200
Non-current investments	1,580	
Non-current (long-term) loan		1,450
	34,507	34,507

You have been given the following further information:

*   The inventories at the close of business on 31 March 20-4 were valued at cost at £4,187,000.

*   Depreciation has been calculated on a monthly basis on all of the non-current assets of the business and has already been entered into the distribution costs and administrative expenses ledger balances as shown on the trial balance.

*   The tax liabilities for the year are £493,000.

*   One of the customers who owed the company £36,000 at the end of the year is in financial difficulties. The directors have estimated that only half of this amount is likely to be paid. No adjustment has been made for this in the accounts. The general provision for doubtful receivables is to be maintained at 2 per cent of the remaining receivables excluding the £36,000 balance.

*   Credit purchases relating to April 20-4 amounting to £265,000 had been entered incorrectly into the accounts in March 20-4.

*   Interest on long-term loan has been paid for six months of the year. No adjustment has been made for the interest due for the final six months of the year. Interest is charged on the loan at a rate of 8 per cent per annum.

*   The land has been revalued by professional valuers at £3,500,000. The revaluation is to be included in the financial statements for the year ended 31 March 20-4.

*   All of the operations are continuing operations.

Task 1.5

Make the necessary journal entries for the year ended 31 March 20-4 as a result of the further information given above. Dates and narratives are not required.

Notes:

1.   You must show any workings relevant to these adjustments.

2.   Ignore any effect of these adjustments on the tax charge for the year given above.

Task 1.6

Making any adjustments required as a result of the further information provided, draft an income statement for the year ending 31 March 20-4, and a balance sheet for Typeset Limited as at that date.

Note: You are *not* required to produce notes to the accounts.

PART C

You are advised to spend about 20 minutes on this part.

DATA

The directors of Typeset Limited, the company in Tasks 1.5 and 1.6, have asked for your assistance in preparing a statement of recognised income and expense.

Task 1.7

(a)   Write a note which explains the purpose of the statement of recognised income and expense.

(b)   Prepare a statement of recognised income and expense for the year ended 31 March 20-4 for Typeset Limited as required by IAS 1.

SECTION 2

You are advised to spend about 55 minutes on this section.

DATA

Magnus Carter has recently inherited a majority shareholding in a company, Baron Limited. The company supplies camping equipment to retail outlets. Magnus wishes to get involved in the management of the business. He would like to understand how the company has performed over the past two years and how efficient it is in using its resources. He has asked you to help him to interpret the financial statements of the company which are set out below.

Baron Limited
Summary Income statement
for the year ended 31 March

	20-4	20-3
	£000	£000
Revenue	1,852	1,691
Cost of sales	(648)	(575)
Gross profit	1,204	1,116
Expenses	(685)	(524)
Profit from operations	519	592
Tax	(125)	(147)
Profit for the year	394	445
Dividends paid in year	325	300

Baron Limited
Summary Balance sheets as at 31 March

	20-4		20-3	
	£000	£000	£000	£000
Non-current assets		1,431		1,393
Current assets				
Inventories	217		159	
Trade receivables	319		236	
Cash and cash equivalents	36		147	
	572		542	
Current liabilities				
Trade payables	(48)		(44)	
Tax liabilities	(125)		(130)	
	(173)		(174)	
Net current assets		399		368
		1,830		1,761
Share capital		1,000		1,000
Retained earnings		830		761
		1,830		1,761

Task 2.1

Prepare a report for Magnus Carter that includes:

(a)   a calculation of the following ratios for the two years:
- gross profit percentage
- net profit percentage
- receivables turnover in days (receivables collection period)
- payables turnover in days (payables payment period, based on cost of sales)
- inventory turnover in days (inventory turnover period, based on cost of sales)

(b)   for each ratio calculated:
- a brief explanation in general terms of the meaning of the ratio
- comments on how the performance or efficiency in the use of resources has changed over the two years

(c)   a statement, with reasons, identifying the areas that could be improved over the next year as indicated by the ratios and analysis performed

Task 2.2

Prepare brief notes to answer for following questions asked by Magnus:

(a)   "Can you please set out the accounting equation for me and explain what is meant by each of the elements?"

(b)   "Please give me two examples of users outside of the company, other than myself and the other shareholders, who may be interested in the financial statements of Baron Limited. For each user can you tell me for what purpose they would use them?"

Unit 11

Drafting financial statements

Practice Examination 4
Aswall plc, Burysane Ltd, Stringberg Ltd, Fieldsomer Ltd

Element coverage

11.1   draft limited company financial statements

11.2   interpret limited company financial statements

Suggested time allocation

Three hours plus fifteen minutes' reading time.

PRACTICE EXAMINATION 4

ASWALL PLC; BURYSANE LTD; STRINGBERG LTD; FIELDSOMER LTD

This Examination is in two sections.

You have to show competence in both sections.

You should therefore attempt and aim to complete every task in both sections.

You should spend about 125 minutes on section 1, and 55 minutes on section 2.

The following pro-formas are given in the Appendix:

- a consolidated balance sheet

- a journal

- a company income statement

- a company cash flow statement

SECTION 1

You should spend about 125 minutes on this section.
This section is in three parts.

PART A
You should spend about 45 minutes on this part.

DATA

The Managing Director of Aswall plc has asked you to prepare the draft consolidated income statement for the group. The company has one subsidiary undertaking, Unsafey Limited. The income statements for the two companies, prepared for internal purposes, for the year ended 31 March 20-4 are set out on the next page.

Income statements for the year ended 31 March 20-4

	Aswall plc	Unsafey Limited
Continuing Operations	£000	£000
Revenue	32,412	12,963
Cost of sales	(14,592)	(5,576)
Gross profit	17,820	7,387
Distribution costs	(5,449)	(1,307)
Administrative expenses	(3,167)	(841)
Dividends received from Unsafey Limited	1,500	–
Profit from operations	10,704	5,239
Finance costs	(1,960)	(980)
Profit before tax	8,744	4,259
Tax	(2,623)	(1,063)
Profit for the year	6,121	3,196

Further information:

- Aswall plc owns 75% of the ordinary share capital of Unsafey Limited.

- During the year Unsafey Limited sold goods which had cost £1,200,000 to Aswall plc for £1,860,000. All of the goods had been sold by Aswall plc by the end of the year.

- Dividends paid during the year were:
      Aswall plc, £3,500,000
      Unsafey Limited, £2,000,000

- There were no impairment losses on goodwill during the year.

Task 1.1

Draft a consolidated income statement for Aswall plc and its subsidiary undertaking for the year ended 31 March 20-4.

DATA

The directors of Aswall plc are considering acquiring another subsidiary undertaking. They have obtained the latest financial statements of the company they wish to purchase and have had some preliminary discussions with the directors of this company. They are unclear about some of the accounting treatments in the financial statements of the company and have asked you to come to a meeting to explain them.

Task 1.2

Prepare notes for a meeting with the directors to explain the accounting treatment of the following issues:

(a)   The company owns the freehold of a building which it constructed for investment purposes. The building is currently rented to another company on commercial terms. The property is not recorded at its historical cost and has not been depreciated.

(b)   A note to the accounts states that there was a fire in the warehouse of the company that occurred after the year end and resulted in considerable losses of non-current assets and inventories. No adjustment for these losses appears to have been made in the year end financial statements.

(c)   There is a non-current liability for something called "deferred tax" in the balance sheet of the company.

Note: You should make reference, where appropriate, to relevant international accounting standards.

PART B

You are advised to spend 50 minutes on this part.

Data

You have been asked to help prepare the financial statements of Burysane Limited for the year ended 31 March 20-4. The extended trial balance of the company as at 31 March 20-4 is shown on the next page.

Further information:

• All of the operations are continuing operations.

• The authorised share capital of the company, all of which has been issued, consists of ordinary shares with a nominal value of £1.

• The corporation tax charge for the year has been calculated as £2,822,000.

• Revenue relating to March 20-4 amounting to £3,200,000 of credit sales had not been entered into the accounts at the year end.

• Interest on the long-term loan has been paid for the first six months of the year. No adjustment has been made for the interest due for the last six months of the year. Interest is charged on the loan at a rate of 8% per annum.

• The land has been revalued by professional valuers at £15,000,000. The revaluation is to be included in the financial statements for the year ended 31 March 20-4.

Task 1.3

Make the necessary journal entries as a result of the further information given above. Dates and narratives are not required.

Note: (1)   You must show any workings relevant to the adjustments.

(2)   Ignore any effect of these adjustments on the tax charge for the year given above.

Task 1.4

(a)   Draft an income statement (including a statement of the change in retained earnings) for Burysane Limited for the year ended 31 March 20-4.

(b)   Draft a balance sheet for Burysane Limited as at 31 March 20-4.

EXTENDED TRIAL BALANCE

BURYSANE LIMITED

31 MARCH 20-4

Description	Trial balance Dr £000	Trial balance Cr £000	Adjustments Dr £000	Adjustments Cr £000	Income statement Dr £000	Income statement Cr £000	Balance sheet Dr £000	Balance sheet Cr £000
Trade payables		2,409						2,409
Prepayments			207				207	
Ordinary share capital		18,000						18,000
Inventories	8,912		9,432	9,432	8,912	9,432	9,432	
Share premium account		6,000						6,000
Administrative expenses	6,143		185	115	6,213			
Distribution costs	9,459		177	92	9,544			
Retained earnings		15,411						15,411
Land – cost	14,000						14,000	
Buildings – cost	12,068						12,068	
Fixtures and fittings – cost	10,217						10,217	
Motor vehicles – cost	18,548						18,548	
Office equipment – cost	3,004						3,004	
Revenue		39,773				39,773		
Trade receivables	1,359						1,359	
Accruals				362				362
Cash and cash equivalents	463						463	
Interest	400				400			
Non-current (long term) loan		10,000						10,000
Buildings – accumulated depreciation		2,603						2,603
Fixtures and fittings – accumulated depreciation		2,754						2,754
Motor vehicles – accumulated depreciation		5,621						5,621
Office equipment – accumulated depreciation		835						835
Purchases	16,858				16,858			
Dividends paid*	2,160				2,160			
Provision for doubtful receivables		185						185
Profit					5,118			5,118
* to be deducted from retained earnings								
TOTAL	103,591	103,591	10,001	10,001	49,205	49,205	69,298	69,298

PART C

You are advised to spend 30 minutes on this part.

DATA

You have been asked to prepare a cash flow statement for Stringberg Limited for the year ended 31 March 20-4. The income statement and balance sheets of Stringberg Limited are set out below.

Stringberg Limited
Income statement for the year ended 31 March 20-4

	£000
Revenue	9,047
Cost of sales	(4,939)
Gross profit	4,108
Gain on the sale of non-current assets	93
Distribution costs	(1,013)
Administrative expenses	(722)
Profit from operations	2,466
Interest paid	(243)
Profit before tax	2,223
Tax	(509)
Profit for the year	1,714

Stringberg Limited
Balance sheet as at 31 March

	20-4		20-3	
	£000	£000	£000	£000
Non-current assets		5,366		4,075
Current assets				
Inventories	3,016		2,284	
Trade receivables	1,508		1,394	
Cash and cash equivalents	23		–	
	4,547		3,678	
Current liabilities				
Trade payables	(1,792)		(1,310)	
Tax liabilities	(509)		(492)	
Bank overdraft	–		(137)	
	(2,301)		(1,939)	
Net current assets		2,246		1,739
Non-current liabilities				
Long-term loan		(3,038)		(3,324)
		4,574		2,490
Equity				
Called up share capital		2,500		1,900
Share premium account		400		–
Retained earnings		1,674		590
Total equity		4,574		2,490

Further information:

- Dividends proposed were: £630,000 in 20-3, and £750,000 in 20-4. These dividends were paid in 20–4 and 20–5 respectively.

- A non-current asset costing £363,000 with accumulated depreciation of £173,000 was sold during the year. The total depreciation charge for the year was £505,000.

- All revenue sales and purchases were on credit. Other expenses were paid for in cash.

Task 1.5

Prepare a reconciliation of profit from operations to net cash flow from operating activities for Stringberg Limited for the year ended 31 March 20-4.

Task 1.6

Prepare a cash flow statement for Stringberg Limited for the year ended 31 March 20-4, in accordance with the requirements of IAS 7.

SECTION 2

You are advised to spend about 55 minutes on this section.

DATA

Maurice Sun plans to invest in Fieldsomer Limited. This is a chain of shops. He is to meet his consultants to discuss the profitability of the company. To prepare for the meeting he has asked you to comment on the change in profitability and the return on capital of the company. He also has some questions about the company's balance sheet. He has given you Fieldsomer's income statements and the summarised balance sheets for the past two years prepared for internal purposes. These are set out below.

Fieldsomer Limited

Summary Income statements for the year ended 31 March

	20-4	20-3
	£000	£000
Revenue	8,420	7,595
Cost of sales	(3,536)	(3,418)
Gross profit	4,884	4,177
Distribution costs	(1,471)	(1,016)
Administrative expenses	(1,224)	(731)
Profit from operations	2,189	2,430
Finance costs	(400)	(480)
Profit before tax	1,789	1,950
Tax	(465)	(569)
Profit for the year	1,324	1,381

Note: dividends paid in 20-4 were £720,000.

Fieldsomer Limited

Balance sheets as at 31 March

	20-4 £000	20-4 £000	20-3 £000	20-3 £000
Non-current assets		15,132		13,880
Current assets	4,624		3,912	
Current liabilities	(2,215)		(1,855)	
Net current assets		2,409		2,057
Non-current (long-term) loan		(5,000)		(6,000)
		12,541		9,937
Equity				
Share capital		6,000		5,000
Share premium account		2,000		1,000
Retained earnings		4,541		3,937
Total equity		12,541		9,937

Task 2.1

Prepare a report for Maurice Sun that includes the following:

(a)   A calculation of the following ratios of Fieldsomer Limited for each of the two years:

(i)   return on capital employed

(ii)   net profit percentage

(iii)   gross profit percentage

(iv)   asset turnover (based on net assets)

(b)   An explanation of the meaning of each ratio and a comment on the performance of Fieldsomer Limited as shown by each of the ratios.

(c)   A conclusion on how the overall performance has changed over the two years.

Task 2.2

Prepare notes for a meeting with Maurice that answers the following questions relating to the balance sheet of Fieldsomer Limited:

(a)   What are the monetary values of the equity, the assets and the liabilities in Fieldsomer Limited as at 31 March 20-4 and how are they related in the accounting equation?

(b)   Why is the final figure of "profit for the year" in the income statement not the same figure that appears as retained earnings on the balance sheet of the company? What, if any, is the connection between the two figures?

Appendix –
photocopiable resources

These pages may be photocopied for student use. It is recommended that they are enlarged to A4 size.

These pages are also available for download from the Resources Section of www.osbornebooks.co.uk

The forms and formats include:

JOURNAL			
Date	Details	Debit £	Credit £

COMPANY INCOME STATEMENT

FOR THE YEAR ENDED ....

£000

Continuing Operations

Revenue

Cost of sales

Gross profit

Distribution costs

Administrative expenses

Profit/(loss) from operations

Finance costs

Profit/(loss) before tax

Tax

Profit/(loss) for the year from continuing operations

Discontinued Operations

Profit/(loss) for the year from discontinued operations

Profit for the year attributable to equity holders

STATEMENT OF RECOGNISED INCOME AND EXPENSE

FOR THE YEAR ENDED ....

£000

Gains/(losses) on revaluation of properties

Tax on items taken directly to equity

Net income recognised directly in equity

    _____

Transfers

Profit/(loss) for the year

    _____

Total recognised income and expense for the year

    _____

COMPANY BALANCE SHEET AS AT ....

£000

Non-current assets

Goodwill

Other intangible assets

Property, plant and equipment

Investments in subsidiaries

Investments in associates

_____

_____

Current assets

Inventories

Trade and other receivables

Cash and cash equivalents

_____

_____

Total assets

_____

Current liabilities

Trade and other payables

Tax liabilities

Bank overdrafts and loans

_____

_____

Net current assets

_____

Non-current liabilities

Bank loans

Long-term provisions

_____

_____

Total liabilities

_____

_____

Net assets

━━━━━

EQUITY

Share capital

Share premium account

Revaluation reserves

Retained earnings

Total equity

_____

━━━━━

COMPANY CASH FLOW STATEMENT

FOR THE YEAR ENDED ....

£000

NET CASH (USED IN)/FROM OPERATING ACTIVITIES

INVESTING ACTIVITIES

NET CASH (USED IN)/FROM INVESTING ACTIVITIES

FINANCING ACTIVITIES

NET CASH (USED IN)/FROM FINANCING ACTIVITIES

NET INCREASE/(DECREASE) IN CASH AND CASH EQUIVALENTS

CASH AND CASH EQUIVALENTS AT BEGINNING OF YEAR

CASH AND CASH EQUIVALENTS AT END OF YEAR

CONSOLIDATED INCOME STATEMENT
FOR THE YEAR ENDED ....

£000

Continuing Operations

Revenue

Cost of sales

Gross profit

Distribution costs

Administrative expenses

Profit/(loss) from operations

Finance costs

Profit/(loss) before tax

Tax

Profit/(loss) for the year from continuing operations

Discontinued Operations

Profit/(loss) for the year from discontinued operations

Profit/(loss) for the year

——

Attributable to:

Equity holders of the parent

Minority interest

——

CONSOLIDATED STATEMENT OF RECOGNISED INCOME AND EXPENSE
FOR THE YEAR ENDED ....

£000

Gains/(losses) on revaluation of properties

Tax on items taken directly to equity

Net income recognised directly in equity

Transfers

Profit/(loss) for the year

Total recognised income and expense for the year

Attributable to:

Equity holders of the parent

Minority interest

CONSOLIDATED BALANCE SHEET AS AT ....

	£000
Non-current assets	
Goodwill	
Other intangible assets	
Property, plant and equipment	
Investments in subsidiaries	
Investments in associates	
	———
	———
Current assets	
Inventories	
Trade and other receivables	
Cash and cash equivalents	
	———
Non-current assets as held for sale	———
Total assets	
	———
Current liabilities	
Trade and other payables	
Tax liabilities	
Bank overdrafts and loans	———
	———
Net current assets	———
Non-current liabilities	
Bank loans	
Long-term provisions	———
	———
Total liabilities	———
Net assets	———
	▬▬▬
EQUITY	
Share capital	
Share premium account	
Revaluation reserves	
Retained earnings	———
Equity attributable to equity holders of the parent	
Minority interest	
Total equity	———
	▬▬▬

REPORT
To:
From:
Subject:
Date:
if required, continue on a separate sheet

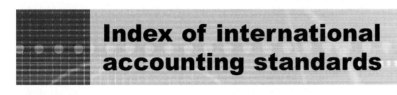

Index of international accounting standards

Page references refer to the text *Limited Company Accounts (IAS) Tutorial.*

International Financial Reporting Standards (IFRSs)

International Accounting Standards (IASs)

continued on the next page

Note: gaps in the numbers represent standards that have been withdrawn

notes

notes

notes

notes